The Green Lanes of Herefordshire

First published 2010
Copyright © 2010 by Heather Hurley
ISBN   978-0-9557577-9-2

 Design: Philip Gray
Walk route maps: Rod Goodman
Typeface: Bembo
FSC   Print: SS Media Ltd
Forest Stewardship Council certified paper

Published by Fineleaf Editions, 2010
Moss Cottage, Pontshill, Ross-on-Wye HR9 5TB
www.fineleaf.co.uk   books@fineleaf.co.uk

British Library Cataloguing in Publication Data
A catalogue record for this book is available from the British Library.

The Green Lanes
of Herefordshire

Heather Hurley

Fineleaf

PUBLISHED BY FINELEAF, ROSS-ON-WYE
www.fineleaf.co.uk

Acknowledgements

With grateful thanks to the staff of the Herefordshire Record Office, the Hereford City Library, the Hereford Cathedral Archives, the Woolhope Club Library, the Bromyard Local History Centre and the Herefordshire Woodlands Latin Group. Also thanks to David Lovelace, Geoff Gwatkin, Brian Smith, Owen Morgan, Mike Mable and Ruth Richardson for help and information. Thanks to the Woolhope Club for funding the colour illustrations from the Geoffrey Walter Smith Fund, to Rod Goodman for reproducing the maps and to Philip Gray of Fineleaf Editions for publishing The Green Lanes of Herefordshire. For accompanying me on exploring the green lanes I wish to thank my husband, Jon, and Fenny and Tara for theirt support.

Text abbreviations

AONB	Area of Outstanding Natural Beauty
ARS	Archaeological Research Section WNFC
BL	British Library
GRO	Gloucestershire Record Office
H JNL	Hereford Journal
HCA	Hereford Cathedral Archives
HCL	Hereford City Library
HT	Hereford Times
HRO	Herefordshire Record Office
HAN	Herefordshire Archaeology News
LOWV	Landscape Origins of the Wye Valley
NMR	National Monuments Record
OS	Ordnance Survey
OSD	Ordnance Survey Draft
RCHM	Royal Commission on Historic Monuments
ROW	Rights of Way
SMR	Sites and Monuments Record
TNA	The National Archives
TWNFC	Transactions of the Woolhope Naturalist's Field Club
WNFC	Woolhope Naturalist Field Club

This book has been published with the support of the Geoffrey Walter Smith Fund of the Woolhope Naturalists' Field Club.

Contents

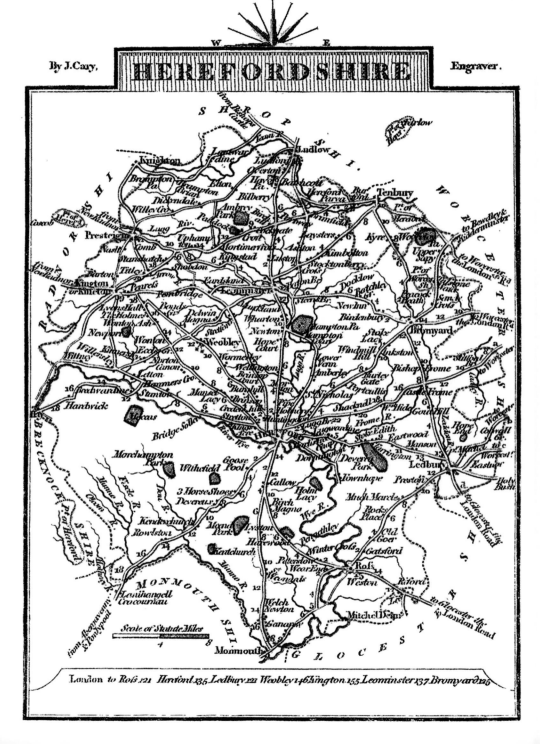

By J.Cary,

HEREFORDSHIRE

Engraver.

London to Ross 121 Hereford 135 Ledbury 122 Weobley 146 Kington 155 Leominster 137 Bromyard 125

Introduction

This book is based on an original piece of research for a paper published in the Woolhope Club's *A Herefordshire Miscellany* in 2000. *The Green Lanes of Herefordshire* expands the subject and focuses on the history and development of ten named lanes spread around the county. Each lane has been thoroughly researched from sources dating from medieval to present day documents, county maps, estate maps, Ordnance Surveys, inclosure awards, road acts, sale particulars, county council records and published works in books and journals. All have been investigated and photographed and recorded to form a comprehensive survey of these lanes.

Green lanes have a wonderfully evocative and rural ring to the words, but the term 'green lanes' is only descriptive and has no legal meaning. Many are defined as rights of way or highways, and those that remain unclassified are currently known as 'lost' with various attempts made to legally define them. Herefordshire retains a wealth of green lanes which vary in character depending on their location and former use. The lanes are usually of carriageway width, partly unsurfaced, often sunken, normally hedged, sometimes banked, occasionally walled and nearly always of historical importance. As green corridors they provide wildlife habitats for varying species of birds, insects, mammals, flora and fauna. The lanes form important features in the landscape and need to be preserved and protected for future generations.

The green lanes featured in the main text have been chosen to represent a county wide selection which have historic origins, interesting features and have survived as footpaths, bridleways or byways forming part of a large network of public rights of way in Herefordshire. To enable these lanes to be appreciated, explored and viewed they have been incorporated into ten circular walking routes following present day lanes and paths. It would be an impossible task to discover and compile a list of all the Herefordshire green lanes, but others known and explored by the author are briefly mentioned in the first chapter as an incentive and encouragement for further research and investigation.

Heather Hurley, Hoarwithy 2010

A map of Herefordshire produced by the cartographer John Cary (1754 - 1835), published in *Cary's Traveller's Companion or a Delineation of the Turnpike Roads of England and Wales*, 1806.

The author riding Explorer on a Harewood bridleway

Cefn Road, Michaelchurch Escley

One
History and Origins

Researching green lanes in Herefordshire has proved to be a challenging task with many hours spent searching for deeds and documents, examining maps and surveys, studying inclosure awards, road acts, sale particulars and published works in books and journals. Of course, the main proof is in the field work, observing the lie of the land, investigating ridgeways, exploring deep hollow-ways which are indicative of a long and constant use and identifying neglected roads from a later period. Many are more difficult to determine their past history without referring to maps, documents and local knowledge.

Herefordshire

The county of Herefordshire, lying along the Welsh Borders, is one of the least spoilt counties in England spreading from the dark heights of the Black Mountains on the west to the rolling hills of the Malverns on its eastern boundary. The higher and wooded ground of north Herefordshire merges into Shropshire, and Gloucestershire's Forest of Dean partly forms its southern boundary. The swift waters of its rivers including the Arrow, Lugg, Frome and Monnow all eventually flow into the Wye, renowned for its picturesque beauty. The fertile soil of the county has encouraged a rich mixture of agriculture, and despite some unsightly modern farming practices, the landscape retains an attractive tapestry of fields, woods, orchards and parks.

Although Herefordshire is one of the smaller populated counties it contains the cathedral city of Hereford and the five market towns of Kington, Leominster, Bromyard, Ledbury and Ross which have grown and developed over the centuries into main centres serving the rural communities. The small villages, tiny hamlets and outlying farms retain a pattern of settlement typical of the Welsh Borders, where the Welsh influence has spread to the place-names. Traditional stone and half-timbered buildings, historic churches, ruined castles, overgrown mottes and wooded hillforts complement the attractive scenery.

In the past travel and transport through Herefordshire relied on a network of tracks and paths that developed according to demand. Over

Vagar Hill, Michaelchurch Escley

Glis Farm 1979, Vagar Hill

GLIS FARM

the centuries these ancient routes became highways, byways or pathways, and as communications improved the important highways were either replaced by more convenient routes or survived to form the basis of our present day road system. This left a legacy in the countryside of byways and pathways, many of which have survived as tracks and hollow-ways dating from prehistoric times to the end of the turnpike era, which form today's green lanes.

In Herefordshire the green lanes vary in character depending on the geology and topography of the area. For example those found on plateaus, river valleys and foothills are usually still enclosed by stock proof hedges, whilst the higher level ones are lined with weathered and crumbling stone walls or steep banks eroded by time. Woodland and forest lanes are difficult to identify due to replanting, forestry work and boundary banks. Ancient routes following ridgeways known as tracks may be included into this category of green lanes, although they are seldom enclosed.

Ridgeways

Ridgeways were established as high level and lengthy routes leading above water courses, often leading to prehistoric sites. In the undulating landscape of Herefordshire ridgeways are not so prominent, and 'it is important to realise that originally they must have looked very different from the way they appear today. They were less pronounced and much wider, as they were only rarely constrained by other features in the landscape'. The ridgeways developed as trading routes and drove roads later enclosed with walls and hedges as farming progressed, therefore many now have the characteristics of green lanes.

Two ridgeways to investigate are located on the foothills of the Black Mountains and can be accessed from Michaelchurch Escley. From the white-washed Methodist chapel of 1866 at Llanrosser a footpath ascends the southern corner of Cefn Hill now defined as 'access land'. Leading south is Cefn Road shown on the current Ordnance Survey, but not marked as a right of way. It is a continuation of a high level ridgeway leading past an earthwork and other sites investigated by the Woolhope Club in 1946 and 1985. In sections the ridgeway 'takes the form of a green lane' which is clearly identifiable on the south western end of the hill.

Running parallel to Cefn Hill is the windswept slopes of Vagar Hill standing at 1420 feet and offering panoramic views. Although in the parish of Michaelchurch Escley it can be reached from Dorstone along the Pitt Road

Watling Street 1888, Leintwardine

Red Rail excavation 2005, Hentland

to Common Bach where an ascent is made to the transmitter mast. Along the ridge a wide and crumbling stone-walled track crosses the open access land as a byway and bridleway leading south to Michaelchurch. Alongside the ridgeway are the remains of Glis Farm probably dating from the late 18th century when occupied by a quarryman. In 1979 more substantial remains of the farm were standing when members of the Woolhope Club made a survey and sketch of this abandoned hill farm.

With knowledge of the landscape combined with studying maps a ridgeway may be identified, although little has survived from its original route. For instance, the ridge walk or ride along the existing bridleway leads from Sellack church and passes ancient sites at Caradoc and Hentland to terminate at Pengethley. The route is now partly enclosed and sunken in places, but past maps and research suggest this is a survivor of a much longer route which forded the Wye at Sellack and followed a similar course to the hillfort at Gaer Cop in Hentland.

Roman Roads

Roman roads are well documented, with routes or probable routes shown on Ordnance Survey maps. The Romans developed an extensive road system which forms the basis of our present pattern, although many sections have fallen into disuse with some stretches surviving as green lanes. Apart from Stone Street in chapter eight, there is a section of Watling Street leading north from Leintwardine, which in 1988 was described as 'easily identified by the sparse and stunted hawthorn hedge'. The course of Watling Street is shown on Ordnance Survey maps and can be traced from the Shropshire borders to Hereford.

In the south of the county a probably Roman road crossed the Wye at Red Rail, along the course of an ancient route that can be traced from Fawley to St. Owens's Cross in Hentland. A short section at Hoarwithy leads along a green lane to the former fording place. Excavation of this road in 2005, by the Landscape Origins of the Wye Valley project, only revealed a paved 18th-century road which may have covered an earlier surface. The approach to the river on the Kings Caple side was excavated in 1969 by the Woolhope Club who concluded it was of Roman construction, and that the lime slabs found scattered in the river probably once formed a causeway or bridge across the Wye. Unfortunately public access on the Kings Caple side had been lost by the mid 19th century, but the remainder of this route can be followed by foot.

Spoon Lane, Dorstone

Packhorse Bridge, Hampton Bishop

Hollow-ways

The most interesting lanes to investigate are those termed as hollow-ways or sunken lanes. Their depth is usually attributed to the constant wear and tear of animals and men, combined with heavy rain washing away the loose soil and stone. It is noticeable that the deepest sections occur on hillsides where excess water flows at its fastest. In the past the surface was 'in a dreadful state, being full of large rocks and loose stones that rendered it dangerous, both to horses and foot passengers'.

The county is traversed by numerous hollow-ways which are regarded as being of medieval origin, but there is a growing evidence that many are of greater antiquity when foot travellers preferred a direct route regardless of steep gradients. Those that have survived should be preserved as 'ancient monuments still in use thousands of years after their creation', and be considered 'as forming a continuous link with prehistoric times'. There are many waiting to be discovered in the Herefordshire countryside, although some have been filled in.

Apart from the hollow-ways covered in the chapters of this book, other examples may be explored. From Rowlestone church a lane marked as Pudding Street in 1835 leads south along a partly tarmaced 'No Through Road' to buildings at Pwll-yr-hunt, where a footpath follows the remnants of an ancient hollow-way. This is deeply sunken in places as it descends to Llancillo Court Farm, with its fascinating motte and isolated church. A further descent leads to the river Monnow where an iron-working forge was leased in 1637 to John Scudamore of Kentchurch and Rowlestone.

In the Golden Valley at Dorstone there is a relatively deep hollow-way known as Spoon Lane leading from the junction of the Hay-on-Wye road with the footpath up to Arthur's Stone. The lane heads in a north westerly direction and formed the turnpike road in 1754 before it was re-routed through the village to its present course. Spoon Lane was impassable in the 1980s but since then the lane has been signed with a red waymark denoting a Public Byway, and forms a section of a British Horse Society's long distance route called the Three Rivers Ride which crosses the Lugg, the Wye and the Usk.

With a keen eye it is easy to recognise hollow-ways which often lead from a medieval site and sometimes form a parish boundary. Those explored by the author include ones at Garway and Harewood associated with the Knights Templar, several at Kentchurch where the Scudamores were based from at least the 12th century, and at Weston-under-Penyard with its remains

Packhorse Inn, Hereford

Pack and Prime Way, Bridstow

of a Norman castle. At Cheyney Court in Bishops Frome, where the former court dated from the 15th century, a footpath which is now part of the Herefordshire Way follows a hollow-way towards Fromes Hill.

Abandoned Roads

Many other green lanes countywide that are of significance, including those that appear to be of ancient origin, were former roads or part of a long distance route, but are difficult to date. On the borders of Monmouthshire at Welsh Newton a footpath leads south from the church through fields to a remaining section of green lane sunken with age and lined with leaning hedges. From a junction of paths the route continues to Mill Farm and Callow Hill before descending to the Mally Brook at Buckholt at the county boundary, where the former Plough Inn with its 'old brewhouse' and 'Cyder Mill' once served travellers until the early 20th century.

At Upton Bishop a green lane leads in a south-westerly direction from cottages at Upton Crews to Felhampton. At its northern end it has recently been defined and signed as a byway, but its southern half which passes Felhampton remains a footpath. On earlier maps it is shown as a through road and was probably used by those avoiding the toll bar at Crow Hill where turnpike roads from Gloucester, Ross and Newent met. Although the toll bar no longer exists there is an almost hidden milestone a few hundred yards south of Crow Hill. It was erected during the turnpike era and is a type of milestone that originally had a plate attached, this has been removed but would have read 'Hereford 13 miles'.

Packhorse Trails

Surviving routes used by packhorses are usually recognisable for being narrower and winding, with a gradual gradient across hilly country where it was more convenient to carry goods by packhorses than by carts or wagons. The names of bridges, lanes and inns associated with packhorses remain as a clue to these routes crossing the county. On Bryant's map of 1835 a long distance route between Holme Lacy and Lugwardine can be traced leading from the Ox Ford over the Wye to Hampton Bishop where the Lugg is crossed by Hampton Bridge, which is known as a packhorse bridge. This old stone and brick structure dates from before 1697 and was repaired by order of Quarter Sessions in 1742 and 1756 as it was an important crossing of the Lugg 'often too deep to ford'. Apart from the stretch from Ox Ford to Hampton Bishop, the remainder of the route has survived as public rights of way.

Former turnpike road at Lea

Turnpike tolls 1782

BREDWARDINE

TOLLS.   By 22d GEO. III.

	s.	d.
FOR every HORSE, or other Beast of Burden, *not drawing* -	0	1.
For every HORSE, or Beast of Burthen, *drawing* any Carriage		3
FOR every SCORE of Cattle - - - - - - -	0	10
FOR every SCORE of CALVES, SWINE, SHEEP, or LAMBS -	0	5

And so in Proportion for any greater, or less Number.

BUT throughout the WHOLE of these Roads, under this Act, no more than 3*d.* can be taken for every Horse, &*c.* not drawing: nor more than 6*d.* for every Horse, &*c.* drawing: nor more than 20*d.* for every Score of Cattle: nor more than 10*d.* for every Score of Calves, Swine, Sheep, or Lambs.

N. B. DOUBLE TOLLs to be taken for all Timber, Lime, Coal and Stone (unless for Repairing the Roads) which shall be haled or drawn along the same, between the first Day of *November,* and the first day of *March.*

In Bridstow parish 'a common and ancient pack and prime way' was recorded at Buckcastle Hill in 1830 by Quarter Sessions. This was one of the lanes which still exist leading past clusters of cottages built on land once belonging to Wilton Manor: from the 1730s this land became the Guy's Hospital Estate. This pack and prime way may date from the 16th century when a weaver was living on 'Buckchastle Hill' and needed his raw materials to be delivered by packhorses. Today the green lane across Buckcastle Hill is approached by narrow footpaths leading from The Woodlands or from Wells Brook Lane.

A number of inns in Herefordshire were known to have been associated with packhorses. There was the 18th century 'Pack Horse' in Leominster, the 'Pack Horse Inn' of the early 19th century at Belmont, and the 18th century 'Pack Horse' in Hereford, which was replaced in 1848 by the Kerry Arms 'erected on the site of the Pack Horse'. In Ross the present Barrel, in Brookend Street, was sold in 1792 and later became the 'Barrel and Woolpack' described in 1813 as a 'Public-House' with 'a kitchen, parlour, large dining-room over the cellar, two good bedrooms, attics and other conveniences'. Its name reflected the two important industries of brewing and woolstapling in Ross.

Drove Ways

From medieval times until the opening of the railways, livestock from Wales were driven to the English markets through Herefordshire towards south east England. After the roads were turnpiked from the 18th century, the drovers preferred to follow byways to avoid the payment of tolls. Green lanes which have been used in the past as drove ways are usually recognisable from their width and grassy verges where cattle could graze, and from field and inn names associated with livestock and drovers. A known drovers' route led from Bredwardine and ascended the slopes of Merbach Hill reaching a height of over 1,000 feet before descending to Middlewood in Clifford. This broad path avoided the toll gates at Bredwardine, and now survives as part of the waymarked Wye Valley Walk.

Approaching Hereford from the west is a wide track leading from Breinton to White Cross and defined partly as a bridleway and byway. It is known as the Green Lane with the adjacent wood and an orchard bearing that name in the mid 19th century. When a woodland reserve was established in 2001 on land alongside the Green Lane it was called Drovers Wood, a name 'chosen through public consultation prior to establishing

An Act for repairing and widening the several
Roads leading into the Town of *Ross* in the
County of *Hereford*.

Whereas the several Roads here- Preamble.
in after-mentioned and describ-
ed, that is to say, the Road
leading from the Town of Ross
in the County of Hereford, to
Harwood's Inn, being Five
Miles, or thereabouts; and also the several Parts of the
Road leading from the said
Town of Ross towards the City of Gloucester (which lie in
the said County of Hereford)
being Five Miles, or thereabouts; and also the Road leading from the Town of Ross aforesaid, to Hoarwithy, being Four Miles, or thereabouts; and also the Road leading from a Place called the Town Brook, in the Town of
Ross aforesaid, to a Place called the Perry Tump in
the Parish of How Caple in the said County of Hereford,
being Four Miles, or thereabouts; and also the Road
leading from the Town Brook aforesaid, to a Place called
the Smith's Shop, in the Parish of Much Marcle, in the
said County of Hereford, being Five Miles, or there-

6 U 2   abouts;

the site' said to derive 'from the use of the bridleway as a route to market for drovers'. A wayside pool opposite is named Drovers Pond, where cattle and horses would have refreshed themselves before reaching the busy streets of Hereford. The Green Lane was a convenient route during the turnpike era, as it avoided the toll bars on the Kings Acre road.

Former turnpikes

After turnpike trusts had been established further acts were required before alterations, improvements and realignments could take place. Along the main route from Gloucester to Hereford, turnpiked in 1726, a number of major alterations were carried out including a new section of road at Lea opened in 1842. This left an abandoned line of turnpike road from the Crown to Castle End which can be followed on foot. From the pub at Lea the old road is tarmaced to Rock Farm and then continues as a wide green lane until rejoining the main road. It was found to be inconvenient for horse-drawn vehicles although it appears to be on dry ground, but the ascent to Rock Farm may have been too steep a gradient. The abandoned road is not shown as a bridleway or byway on the present Ordnance Survey but is regularly walked and ridden.

There are many other examples in Herefordshire of abandoned stretches of toll roads, some were closed by Quarter Sessions, others remained open as byways and many have been preserved as public rights-of way. From 1730 the Hereford Trust turnpiked a network of roads including one through Holme Lacy to 'Hoar Withy Passage' which was partly replaced by a 'new road' after the Road Act of 1789. The new route avoided the hills and left sections of former roads still visible today. A typical stretch may be explored from the inn at Carey in Ballingham. Now defined as a footpath it follows the line of the former turnpike, and as it ascends a sunken and overgrown section is visible from the dry-weather path above.

Bridle roads

Bridle Road as a descriptive term or a name on maps and plans appears to date from the turnpike era. In 1835 Bryant produced his county map of Herefordshire with numerous narrow and double-lined routes marked as Bridle Roads. When checked on present Ordnance Survey maps few have survived; some are demoted to footpaths while others are now defined as bridleways. At Yarkhill a Bridle Road marked by Bryant in 1835 led from Monkhide Mill to Stretton Grandison and has remained as a bridleway, although the surrounding

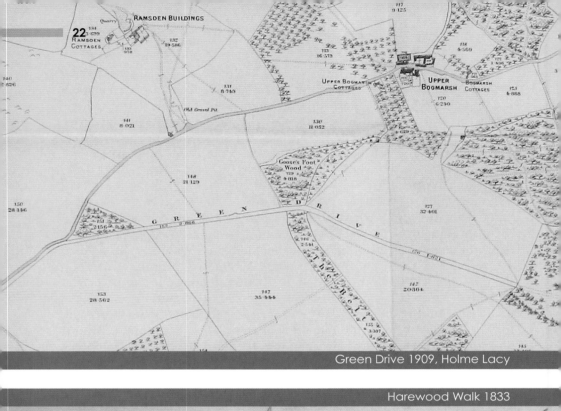

Green Drive 1909, Holme Lacy

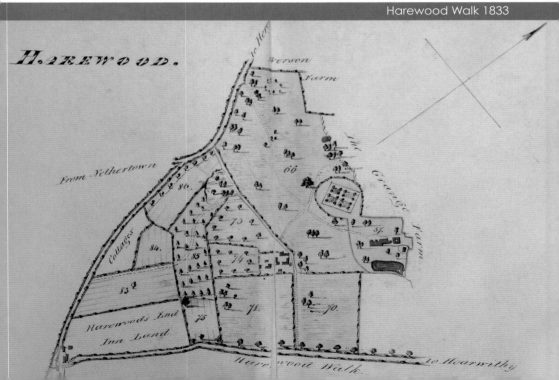

Harewood Walk 1833

landscape was dramatically changed in the 1840s when the Hereford to Gloucester Canal was extended and the corn mill fell into dis-use.

In 1837 a Parliamentary Paper featured 'Conventional Signs to be used in the Plans made under the Act for the Commutation of Tithes' showing a bold line for Bridle Roads. This was followed by Ordnance Survey publishing 'Instructions to Field Examiners' in 1907, with a list including Bridle Roads. Since then the term has been replaced by bridleway, although 'bridle way' was used by Ogilby in his Britannia of 1675 'to Hereford ye bridle way' from Bridstow which was a route later turnpiked in 1749 by the Ross Trustees from 'the Town of Ross aforesaid, to Hoarwithy, being four miles, or thereabout'.

Lane names

From the mid-19th century tithe maps, at least 30 Green Lanes were listed, plus several Greenways and a host of interesting names such as Feather Bed Lane, Brimfield; Tinkler Lane, Cradley; Bear Lane, Dorstone; Coppermarsh Lane, Hampton Bishop; Darkie Lane, Llanveynoe and Far Barnett Lane in Wigmore. A hundred years later Herefordshire Council listed unclassified roads which included an interesting selection of names: Fishpool Lane, Pencoyd; Shop Lane, Goodrich; Barrel Lane, Aston Ingham; Bargains Lane, Little Marcle; Gipsy Lane in Brobury and the legendry Dead Woman at Kinsham. Since being listed some have been lost, others have survived as rights of way or unclassified roads which are usually tarmaced. Betzdorf Walk in Ross is a name given to a former section of the Ross to Monmouth Railway, and other dis-used railway lines may be considered as green lanes in the future.

Researching past names is adequately described in the following chapters, but others of interest that have been investigated by the author include those with river connections. Old Wharf Lane at Whitchurch leads to the River Wye where the wharf is still used by pleasure boats, and when work was carried out a few years ago there was evidence of it being used as a coal wharf, probably for the local lime burning industry. Unfortunately due to developments along the riverside, the lane's hedges have been partly removed since appearing on maps of 1847 and 1862.

A green lane of carriageway width known as Ford Road leads to a former river crossing at Ballingham, which dates from at least the 18th century. From the end of its enclosed section it continues as a field path leading to the railway remains at Careybridge, formerly known as Careyboat when the ferry was in use. At Fownhope a lane signed as Ferry Lane leads onto a short

Llanfrother Lane, Hentland

Altbough Lane, Hentland

section of green lane which once led to the ferry that conveyed passengers across to Holme Lacy until about 1924. The lane also accessed a Coal Wharf at the Locken Stock field, recorded in 1763.

Estate maps, plans and sale particulars are another useful source for names of drives, rides and walks that have survived as green lanes. The Monnington Walk is a wide avenue of pines and yews, probably planted around 1650, leading from the Court to Brobury Scar mapped in 1771. It would have been used as a ride with plenty of width to enjoy an exhilarating gallop, and is now a bridleway forming a delightful stretch of the Wye Valley Walk. At Holme Lacy the Scudamores in the late 18th century created a Green Drive from Holme Lacy House to Newtown which remains as a footpath today, and at Harewood the Hoskyns marked the Harewood Walk on their estate map of 1833.

Lost Lanes

In Herefordshire there are existing green lanes that have never been defined as roads or rights of way that are currently known as Lost Ways. Since the National Parks and Access to the Countryside Act of 1949 various attempts have been sought to add unclaimed lanes to the definitive map. The Discovering Lost Ways project of 2001 failed due to 'not adding a single path to the rights of way network' and being 'extremely resource intensive'. In 2010 Natural England published their Stepping Forward report in the hope of speeding up the lengthy and legal process of adding unclaimed green lanes to the definitive map, which will be lost if not claimed before 2026.

Many individuals and council employees have spent time and resources in researching unclaimed lanes. Those known to have been researched are the Cefn Road at Michaelchurch Escley, already mentioned in this chapter, the Green Lane at Orcop, Hell's Ditch at Peterstow, Llanfrother Lane and Altbough Lane in Hentland parish, Boat Lane at Walford and Goodrich and a lane to the mast on Garway Hill. According to Herefordshire Council in 2010 'given recent developments (political and financial)' they 'don't imagine that reviewing definitive map procedures will be especially high on the Government's agenda for legislative reform'.

Sources

Books
- *D Whitehead and J Eisel, A Herefordshire Miscellany, Woolhope Club, 2000*
- *H Hurley, The Old Roads of South Herefordshire 2nd ed 2007*
- *C Heath, Excursion Down the Wye, 1804*
- *J Webb, Memorials of the Civil War 1879*
- *P Hindle, Roads and Tracks 2001*
- *S Coates & D Tucker, Water-Mills of the Monnow & Trothy 1978*
- *Herefordshire Directories 1902, 1867*
- *D Whitehead, A Survey of Historic Parks and Gardens in Herefordshire 2001*
- *D Whitehead, Survey of Holme Lacy 2003 HCL 712.6*
- *J H Turner, Herefordshire Treasures 1981*
- *H & J Hurley, Rambles & Refreshments on the Welsh Borders 1988*
- *H Hurley ed., Landscape Origins of the Wye Valley 2008*
- *H Hurley, The Pubs of Monmouth, Chepstow and the Wye Valley 2007*
- *A Brian, Six Walks Exploring the Lower Lugg 1993*
- *H Hurley, The Pubs of Ross and South Herefordshire 2001*
- *H & J Hurley, The Wye Valley Walk 1994*
- *R Shoesmith & J Eisel, The Pubs of Hereford City 2004*
- *J Eisel & R Shoesmith, The Pubs of Bromyard and Ledbury 2003*
- *R Shoesmith & R Barrett, The Pubs of Leominster and Kington 2000*
- *Herefordshire Council Unclassified Roads 1936*
- *B Smith, Herefordshire Maps 2004*
- *S Taylor, What is a Cross Road 1997*
- *V Belsey, The Green Lanes of England 1998*

Maps
- *Taylor 1754, 1763*
- *Bryant 1835*
- *G Gwatkin, copies of Parish Tithe Maps*
- *Price 1817*
- *OSD 1814-1817, OS 1831, 1888, 2006*
- *Guys Estate, Wilton Manor 1755 HRO C59/6*
- *Washings Farm Sale 1862 HRO E40/28*
- *Whitworth Survey 1779*

- *Holme Lacy Sale 1909 HCL 914.244*
- *Monnington Court Estate Map 1771 Woolhope Club Library*
- *Harewood Estate map 1833 HRO AW22/1*
- *OS, South Hereford c1920*
- *Kentchurch Archive, LOWV Archive HRO*

Journals/Acts
- *HAN 36 1979, 44 1985*
- *TWNFC 1946*
- *Ross Road Act 1749*
- *H Hurley, Deadwoman Deeds in preparation*

Websites
- *Herefordshire Equestrian www.herefordequestrian.co.uk*
- *Clifford Parish www.cliffordparish.org.uk*
- *Woodland Trust woodlandtrust.org.uk*
- *Herefordshire Sites and Monuments www.smr.herefordshire.gov.uk*
- *Country Landowners Association www.cla.org.uk*
- *Ramblers' Association www.ramblers.org.uk*
- *Institute Public Rights of Way www.iprow.co.uk/gpg/index.php/discovering_lost_ways*
- *Natural England www.naturalengland.org.uk*

Enlarged extract from Ordnance Survey First Edition 1 inch to 1 mile map (Old Series) 1831

Two

Bridge Lane, Wellington

From the outskirts of Wellington Village the southern end of Bridge Lane has the physical characteristics of an ancient route; it is sunken, unsurfaced and of carriageway width as it ascends Wellington Woods. Along the top of its western bank the 'dry weather path' runs above, a typical feature of the old roads in Herefordshire which frequently became 'impenetrable, impassable, churned into mud by horse's hooves and deeply rutted by wheeled vehicles'. Over the centuries the heavy use of the lane led to alternative tracks established to convey the stone from the quarries, lime from the kilns and timber from the coppices in Wellington Wood.

Beyond Hill Cottage and north of the quarries the line of the lane is less sunken, and levels out over the brow of the hill. From the edge of Wellington Woods to Brickyard Cottage the field path follows the boundary between the parishes of Dinmore and Canon Pyon. Beyond this cottage to The Cotts Farm there is plenty of evidence to suggest the course of a former lane, and between the cottages at Westhope 'there is still some common land and a maze of green lanes' which are lined with thick hedges of holly, blackthorn, ivy and elder. The only other green lane which features in this chapter is joined at Derndale Hill, and was probably known as Wood Lane – the same name as an adjoining field.

History

In the mid-19th century Wellington was described as 'a long straggling village, delightfully situated in a vale, surrounded by hills', but it was in the hills that the earliest settlements were established. In Wellington Woods a rectangular earthwork has been identified, which may have been the site of a building associated with huntsmen or herdsmen. According to tradition a homestead moat and stone masonry near The Cotts Farm was the site of a chapel and a depopulated place known anciently as Smethley. When visited by the Woolhope Club they suggested that it had once been a fortified residence.

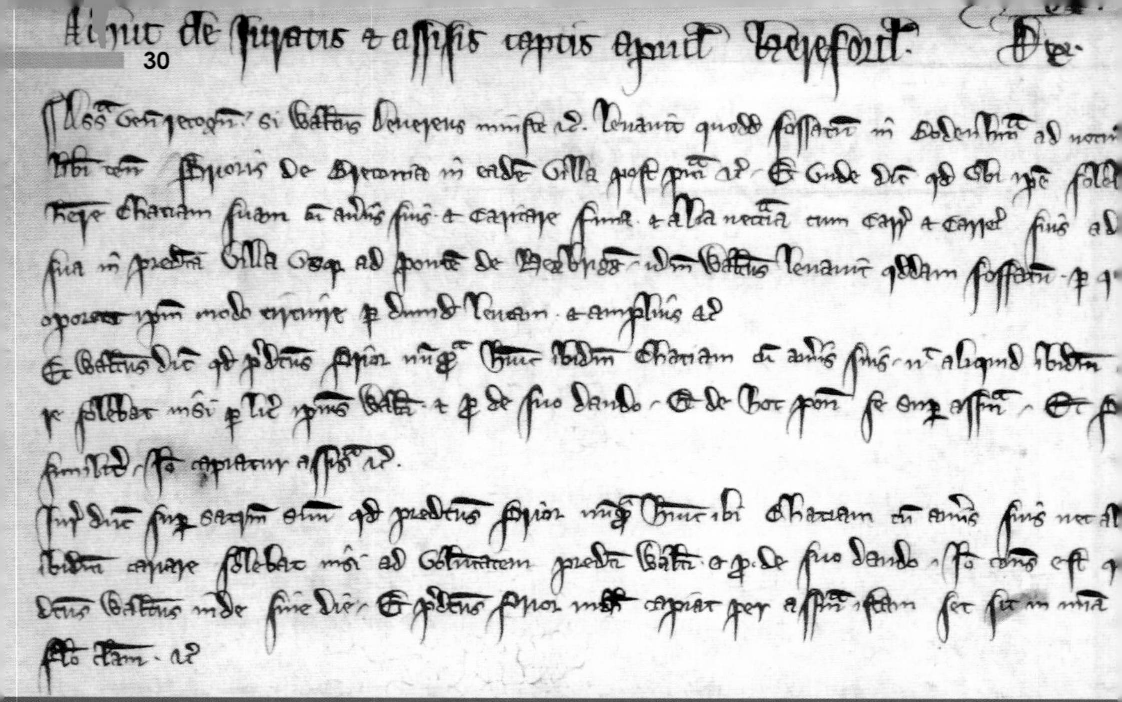

Wellington Assize Roll 1293

Wellington village 1883

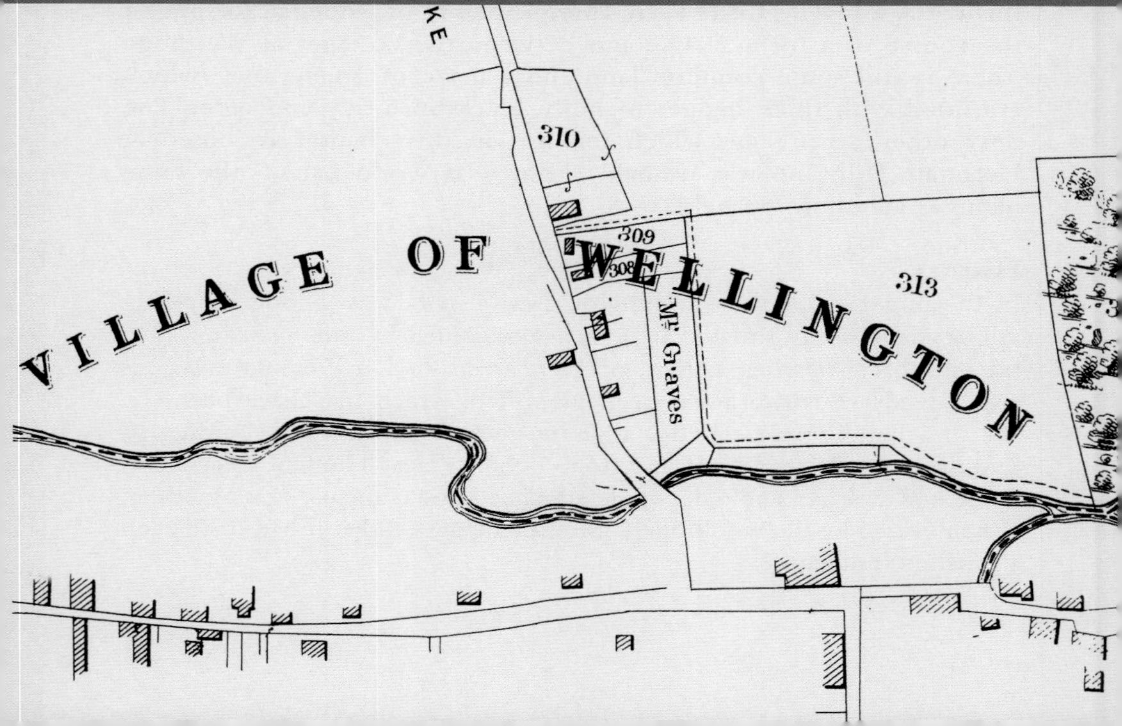

VILLAGE OF WELLINGTON

310

309
308

313

Mr Graves

KE

In the 12th century 'half of Wellington Wood' belonged to the Knights Hospitallers at Dinmore, and the southern part was held by Robert Chandos. In 1163 he 'was ordered by the Bishop of Hereford to allow the parson of Wellington church access to the Manor's woods for his fuel needs, fencing material and cattle pasture', and 1n 1293 the court had to decide whether Robert Chandos had 'unjustly stopped access to a certain roadway in Wellington' preventing Richard Baggingdon access from his house in Wellington to Robert's woodland where he had 'rights to collect wood for domestic repairs, mending hedges and firewood which he carries and carts from the woodland to his house'. After the case was heard the jury decided he had not been affected so he was convicted 'for bringing a false claim'.

In 1675 the Brydges family of the Ley held 30 acres of land known as Bridge Wood in the northern end of Wellington Wood, where ditches and banks indicate parish boundaries. A Bargain and Sale of 1700 recites that 'Bridges Wood in parish of Wellington' was covenanted from Symon Brydges to his servant who 'performed his duties faithfully'. It may be that Bridge Lane was named after this family as its first known record in 1726 was long before the bridge was built to replace the ford across the Wellington Brook.

At the village end of Bridge Lane, the older properties all date from the early 18th century, one of which may have developed from the 'messuage with barn, outhouses, garden and orchard containing 1½ acres in Bridge Lane' the home of Thomas Jones in 1726. Another property was described in 1756 as 'a cottage in Bridge Lane, Wellington, with barn, garden, orchard etc. containing 1 acre' together with 'a cottage with appurtenances in Bridge Lane, adjoining the barn'. Both had arable in the common fields and seats in Wellington Church. These may have been the '2 messuages late Robinsons' recorded in 1792.

In 1811 an assessment of six pence in the pound was charged upon the 'Occupiers of Lands Tenements Woods or Tithes and Hereditments within the Parish of Wellington'. In Bridge Lane the following inhabitants were eligible to pay - Thomas Baldwin, James Godwin, John Beavan, William Graves, William Mason, William Evans and W. Beavan. Once collected the amount went 'towards the amendments and preservation of the Highways within the Parish'.

In the mid-19th century there were at least twelve cottages, houses and one smithy with gardens and orchards situated between the ford in Bridge Lane and the road it crosses known as North Field Lane. There was

Bridge Lane, Wellington 2009

Bridge Lane 1905

also the elusive Globe Inn, a beer house at an unidentified site thought to be in Bridge Lane. It has been suggested 'that there was a decree during the reign of Queen Victoria that foresters should not have to travel more than a mile for their lunchtime cider – hence the many cider houses in remote cottages in the woods'.

The Wellington Court estate was offered for sale in 1883 with its 670 acres, which included a few cottages in Bridge Lane and woodland at Chance Hill in Wellington Woods where a 'Stone Quarry' was still providing 'some very good Metal'. This would have been transported down Bridge Lane around the time that a footbridge made of railway sleepers crossed the brook alongside the ford, and was photographed in 1905. It was not until the mid-20th century that the ford and footbridge was replaced by a county bridge and that the unsurfaced section of Bridge Lane was defined as a public footpath lying along the 'top of S.W. side of sunken lane at commencement and not up centre of lane'.

Exploring Bridge Lane

From the attractive village of Wellington this route follows Bridge Lane which ascends through Wellington Woods to open farmland offering panoramic views. From Brickyard Cottage the scanty remains of a former green lane will be identified before reaching Westhope, where a maze of lanes may be explored before returning along field paths and a sunken lane. At the time of writing all the paths were signed or waymarked, and some sections were muddy.

Length	**7 miles**
OS Map	**Explorer 202**
Start	**Bridge Lane, Wellington** (8 miles south of Leominster on the A49)
Parking	**Village Centre GR494482** – signed from A49
Refreshments	**Wellington Inn (01432 830367), Wellington**
Public transport	**492 bus (Lugg Valley) Leominster to Hereford**

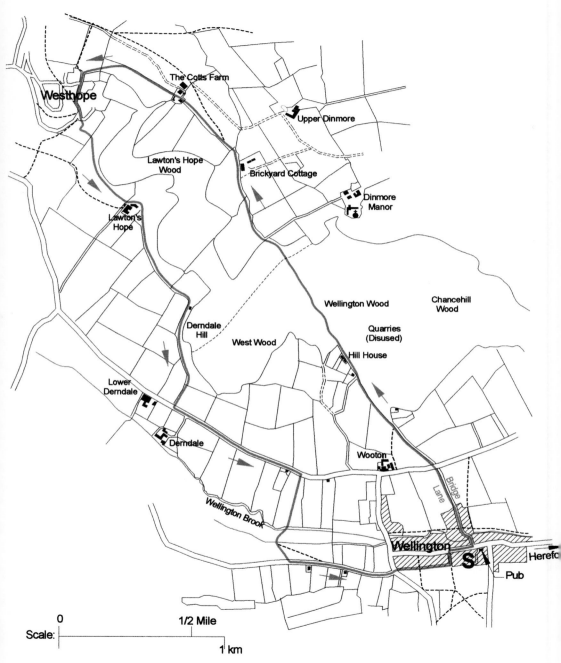

Westhope
The Cotts Farm
Upper Dinmore
Lawton's Hope
Wood
Brickyard Cottage
Dinmore
Manor
Lawton's
Hope
Wellington Wood
Chancehill
Wood
Derndale
Hill
Quarries
(Disused)
West Wood
Hill House
Lower
Derndale
Derndale
Wooton
Bridge Lane
Wellington Brook
Wellington
S
Hereford
Pub

0   1/2 Mile
Scale:
                              1 km

Circular Route

Almost opposite the post office follow Bridge Lane, which starts as a tarmac lane and leads north from the village street. A mixture of old and new properties line the lane which crosses the Wellington Brook and continues ahead as a sunken lane, where the waymarked right of way leads above on the left-hand bank as a 'dry weather path'. At the minor crossroads keep ahead following the signed path above the deeply sunken green lane which can be investigated at intervals.

At Hill House the lane is joined leading to a series of steps into Wellington Wood, where the woodland path ascends to a stile and continues ahead through open farmland to Brickyard Cottage near Upper Dinmore. From there the footpath follows the identifiable route of a former lane past Cotts Farm towards Westhope. Further on a stile on the left should not be missed, where the path descends a field diagonally right to a pair of stiles on the eastern outskirts of Westhope.

A delightful sunken lane leads down to a property called Backwoods in Westhope, where a finger post directs the way to another prominent finger post at the junction of a maze of lanes signed as footpaths or byways. The footpath goes left along a sunken lane to Folly Hall Cottage and down a flight of steps to a stile and the start of a field path. This field path zigzags as directed across the fields below Lawton's Hope Wood and through the farmyard at Lawton's Hope.

The farm house at Lawton's Hope is timber-framed and dates from the late 17th century with documentation showing that it had once 'enjoyed gentry occupation'. From the farmyard the way needs to be checked to insure the correct route of the path is followed along the contour line to an orchard and a cottage below the woods of Derndale Hill. The right of way partly follows a green lane and a path through an orchard to reach the road at Derndale near Wellington.

Turn left along the road for approximately half a mile, and just beyond a cottage and barn follow a signed footpath on the right through fields and over the Wellington Brook and then a ditch to reach the road followed left to a junction. Ascend the steps opposite to follow a narrow path which runs along the back of the village houses, and take the second footpath on the left to return to the village street.

36

Byway sign, Westhope

Steps in Wellington Wood

Sources

Books
- *H. Hurley, The Green Lanes of Herefordshire, A Herefordshire Miscellany 2000*
- *L. Pugh, Westhope 1988*
- *J. Webb, Memorials of the Civil War 1879*
- *Herefordshire Directory 1858*
- *C. Robinson, The Mansions and Manors of Herefordshire 1872*
- *R. Shoesmith & R. Barrett, The Pubs of Leominster 2000*
- *D. Whitehead, A Survey of Historic Parks and Gardens in Herefordshire 2001*
- *RCHM 1932*

Archives
- *D. Lovelace, Woods of the Dinmore Estate mss. 2000*
- *Sale Particulars 1883, HRO N78/45*
- *Bargain and Sale 1700, HRO F78/11/135*
- *Wellington Highways assessment 1811, HCA 4324*
- *Wellington Wood Case 1293, TNA Just1/302*
- *Mandate to Robert de Chandos 1163, HCA 1385*
- *Dean and Chapter Grant 1188, HCA 487*
- *Mortgage 1726, HRO L48/45*
- *Relase and Mortgage 1756, HRO L48/46*
- *Mortgage 1792, HRO N51/11*

Maps
- *Wellington Tithe Map 1843*
- *OSD 1817, OS 1831, 1888, 2006*
- *Bryant 1835*
- *Wellington Definitive Map 1952, HRO*

Websites
- *Wellington History Society wellingtonhistory.org.uk*
- *Herefordshire Sites and Monuments www.smr.herefordshire.gov.uk*

Enlarged extract from Ordnance Survey First Edition 1 inch to 1 mile map (Old Series) 1831

Three
Stockton Ride, Kimbolton

The first section along the Stockton Ride ascends a deep banked green lane, showing evidence of the wear and weathering of an ancient route which once forked westwards towards Ratefield Farm. The banks are draped with ivy below the oaks, birch, holly and hazel of the long strip of woodland known earlier as The Ride. From a cottage called The Ryde the green lane levels and narrows as it pleasantly skirts the east side of the wood. Further along it leads through a gate into fields outside the wooded Ride, where stretches of partly broken iron fencing are the remains of palling erected in the 1890s. The fence lies twisted and leans on trees marking an eastern boundary of the Berrington Hall estate.

From gaps in the hedges and between mature trees, it is possible to discover that another track runs parallel through the middle of the wooded strip. From earlier maps and plans this only existed from the late 19th century and appears to be overgrown. The route of today's footpath along the Stockton Ride has not changed since first shown on early 19th century maps when it undoubtedly formed a route for a pleasure ride or drive around the Berrington Hall estate. It may have formed a continuation of the Morton Ride, running along the western edge of Berrington Park.

History
In 1857 Kimbolton was described as 'a large straggling parish, with the townships of Stockton and Hamnish Clifford, 2½ miles north-east from Leominster station, 15 from Hereford, situated on rising ground, and on the turnpike road from Leominster to Tenbury'. Lord Rodney of Berrington Hall was one of the principle landowners who owned a large portion of Kimbolton which included land at Hawthorn, Upper Kimbolton and the Stockton Ride. In 1775 Berrington Hall had been purchased by Thomas Harley who began to improve the estate with the help of Capability Brown. Further enhancements were made after 1781 when Harley's daughter married Lord Rodney who eventually inherited the large estate in 1804 and it was probably his family that created the Stockton Ride on his land in Kimbolton.

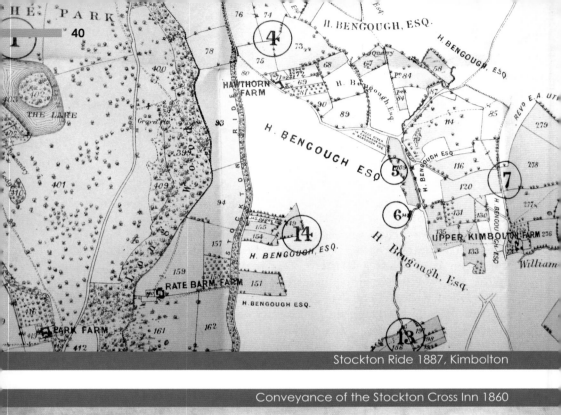

Stockton Ride 1887, Kimbolton

Conveyance of the Stockton Cross Inn 1860

Dated 22nd March 1860

The Revd E. A. Uthwatt and wife and others

to

Mr William Phillips

Appointment and Conveyance of two undivided moieties being the entirety of Stockton Cross Farm in the parish of Kimbolton Herefordshire

The names of the Stockton and Morton Rides suggest they must have evolved as pleasure rides or carriage drives to view the extensive park. Although planted at a later date than other rides, walks and avenues in Herefordshire parks, it was a fashionable pursuit to entertain guests on horseback or by carriage to view the estate. The earliest known existence of the Stockton Ride dates from the first edition of the Ordnance Survey, where the belt of trees is marked and named The Ride leading north from Stockton to Ashton.

From the mid 19th century The Ride was well established. It passed three cottages along the way; two owned by Edward Bowdley of Lower Kimbolton, and the other by Thomas Marshall, before reaching the turn east to Hawthorn Farm owned by Lord Rodney. Hawthorn Farm was recorded as 'newly erected' in 1887 and was for sale with its 83 acres. In 1925 its sale particulars included the sale of 'A Small Holding known as The Ride' which was a stone built cottage with a garden and two pieces of pasture let at a rent of £6 a year.

It was not until 1888 that the Stockton Ride was named on maps, and has been ever since. The 1904 survey clearly shows the Stockton and Morton Rides. In 1952 the Herefordshire County Council Rights of Way approved and accepted the route along the Stockton Ride from 'Stockton Cross Inn to Parish Boundary with Ashton' as a footpath, given the number 1 in Kimbolton parish. At that date the route was 'blocked in a few places by fallen trees', but when investigated in the mid 1980s there was some confusion along the correct route before the council waymarked the path. Fortunately for riders the Morton Ride in Eye parish was given a more acceptable status of a bridleway.

The northern end of the Stockton Ride leads to The Hundred where leases of 'tenements and land at ye Hundred' date from 1711, and The Hundred Farm was 'A Desirable Small Dairy Farm' with 47 acres in 1887. Beyond the minor crossroads another green lane preserved as a public footpath winds north along an unsurfaced lane of carriageway width. It starts as an enclosed lane but its hedges have been partly removed before reaching Middleton on the Hill, where according to earlier maps many lanes have been downgraded to footpath status. Field names suggest that one of these lanes was known as Norman Lane.

Middleton church dates from the 12th century, and Middleton Farm from the 17th century which together with Church House Farm are situated at the end of a 'no through road'. A number of footpaths lead to the church

Stockton Ride fencing

Stockton and Morton Rides 1888

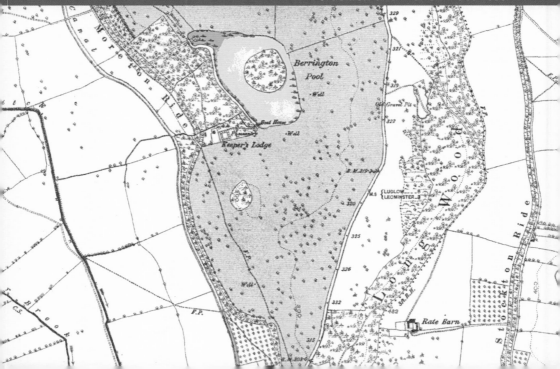

indicating a place of past importance, where a medieval village has been identified. Church House Farm, formerly Church Farm, was described as being 'recently constructed' in 1887 when owned by the Berrington Hall estate. Also within Middleton parish is an extensive range of farm buildings at The Rock which enjoys a long documented history from the late 17th century.

From Town Farm footpaths follow the course of an enclosed lane, but hedges had been partly removed by the mid 19th century. Before reaching Upper Kimbolton a rather muddy and rocky lane has survived which connects the present field path to a tarmac lane at Kimbolton with its prominent church spire. At Stockton its pub was conveniently placed to catch trade on two important roads, one leading from Tenbury to Stockton Cross that was turnpiked in 1737 and the other turnpiked by the Leominster Trust in 1729 leading from 'the Mill in the Mill Street, in the said town to Stockton'. The inn was kept by the Phillips family when owned by the Rev Utwhatt, who sold the 'Public House Orchard and Garden' in 1860. It was acquired by the Ross based Alton Court Brewery in 1900 and has since remained open offering hospitality and substance.

Exploring Stockton Ride

Stockton is a scattered hamlet in the large parish of Kimbolton lying north of Leominster. The Stockton Cross Inn forms a prominent landmark and the start of an easy and most enjoyable ramble along at least two miles of the Stockton Ride which is partly enclosed as a green lane before entering open fields and offering fine views. From a cluster of farms and cottages at The Hundred the tarmac lane leads to the start of another green lane signed as a footpath and leading north to Middleton on the Hill.

Length	**8.5 miles**
OS Map	**Explorer 203**
Start	**Stockton Cross Inn GR519612, Kimbolton**
Parking	**Along the road near the inn**
Refreshment	**Stockton Cross Inn (01568 612509), Kimbolton**
Public Transport	**Infrequent bus service**

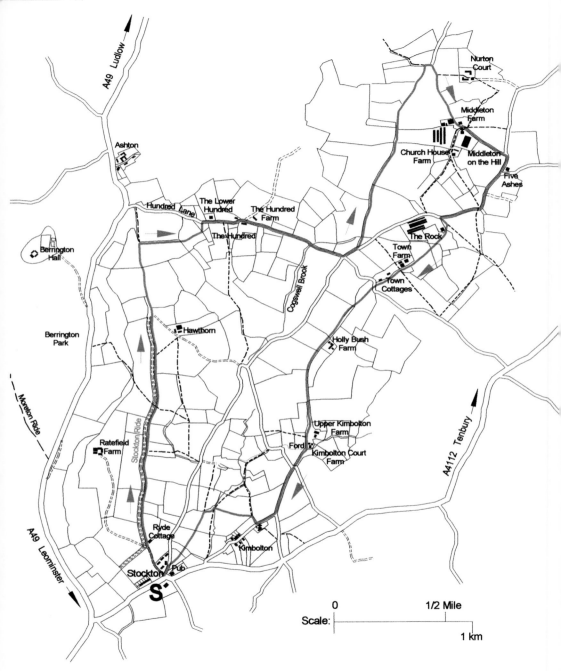

A49 Ludlow

Ashton

Hundred Lane
The Lower Hundred
The Hundred Farm
The Hundred

Berrington Hall

Berrington Park

Hawthorn

Moreton Ride

Ratefield Farm

Stockton Ride

Ryde Cottage

A49 Leominster

Stockton
Pub

S

Kimbolton

Upper Kimbolton Farm
Ford
Kimbolton Court Farm

Holly Bush Farm

Cogswell Brook

Nurton Court

Middleton Farm

Church House Farm
Middleton on the Hill

Five Ashes

The Rock

Town Farm

Town Cottages

A4112 Tenbury

Scale:
0   1/2 Mile
                   1 km

Circular Route

Opposite the Stockton Cross Inn a signed footpath directs the way along a sunken green lane following the Stockton Ride through a strip of woodland. It ascends gently below steep banks to pass a cottage called The Ryde, then alongside a narrowing strip of trees. A gate leads into open fields where the footpath continues ahead passing two signed paths to Hawthorn Farm seen in the distance. The next footpath on the right is followed through fields to access the road at The Hundred.

The quiet road known as Hundred Lane dips down to a crossroads, where a left turn is followed for a few hundred yards towards Middleton on the Hill. Then follow the first green lane on the left signed as a public footpath which heads north for about one and a half miles. It is partly enclosed but hedges have been removed along some sections, providing views of Middleton on the Hill. On reaching a junction of lanes keep right following the fingerposts, but do not miss the signed field path to the church at Middleton.

Clusters of ancient and modern farm buildings, belonging to Middleton Farm and Church House Farm, surround the attractive church where a mounting block is a reminder of travel by horseback. From the church a tarmac lane leads straight to the road where a right turn is followed to a half timbered cottage at Five Ashes. Continue around the bends to a signed footpath beside the drive to The Rock. The path enters the field then turns right behind the buildings and ahead over stiles and through fields to Town Farm.

From Town Farm the path follows a track to the road, where at the time of writing an unsigned field path skirts Holly Bush Farm and continues to Upper Kimbolton Farm. Prior to reaching this farm the path enters a green lane defined as a byway which crosses a ford and follows a tarmac lane to the church at Kimbolton. Opposite the church a signed field path traverses fields and over a succession of stiles in an easterly then southern direction to reach the minor road at Stockton and the Stockton Cross Inn.

Church at Middleton on the Hill

Signpost at Middleton on the Hill

Sources

Books
- *D Whitehead, A Survey of Historic Parks and Gardens 2001*
- *H & J Hurley, Rambles and Refreshments 1988*
- *Herefordshire Directories 1857, 1867, 1902*
- *J Richardson, The Local Historian's Encyclopedia 1989*
- *A & S Davis, and A & T Malpas, The Book of Kimbolton 1986*

Archives
- *Pateshall sale 1917 HRO M5/6/60*
- *National Trust, Berrington Hall 1958 HCL*
- *Hawthorn sale 1925 HRO M5/16/15*
- *Kimbolton ROW 1952 HRO CD31/27*
- *Middleton on the Hill ROW 1952 HRO CD31/29*
- *Leases of The Hundred 1711 HRO A63/III/11/8*
- *Berrington Hall sale 1887 HRO M5/8/40*
- *Tenbury Turnpike Act 1737 HRO W20/12*
- *Leominster Turnpike Act 1729 HRO BO11/1*
- *Stockton Cross Inn 1860 - 1904 HRO BD29/10/1-8*
- *The Rock leases HRO A63/III/13*

Maps
- *Kimbolton Tithe Map 1841*
- *Middleton on the Hill Tithe Map 1841*
- *OS 1831, 1888, 1904, 2006*
- *Bryant 1835*
- *Price 1817*

Websites
- *Herefordshire Sites and Monuments www.smr.herefordshire.gov.uk*

48

Thornbury Stonehouse Stoney Bridge
Will perry
Hubbage Bank Fieldhouse PART OF Tedstone Wafre
Mill Rowgrove The Hill Hope Farm Court
Streetfield E d v i n s WORCESTERSHIRE
Upper Horton W o o d Camp House Edvin Loach
Butterly building Lower Horton Old house Steeles
Upper House Saltmarsh
Sunderland Grun Parsonage Brick house Wilbatch Little B
Lower House Blackvan Newhouse Mic
Wackton Pound Farm Brookhouse
Upper Wackton Edvin Ralph
Little Wackton Park Farm Broomhill
Wackton Farm Tuck Farm Old Mill
Rowden Mill Turkeyhall Sandy Close
Peacocks Heath Buckenhill
Rowden Landywool Broad Oak Hillhou
Wickton Rock Rainsford Ravensnest
Boulters close Watteron New Barns Bromyard
Red Hill Hardwick Inkstone Bridge Rhee
Sawbury Hill Hardwick Mill Oldhouse Walk Mill Drewe
Vouks Three Mills Warr
Mill House Broad Bridge
Munderfield Harold The Fire BROMYARD Brick Barn
Stonehouse Hodgbatch
The Green Flaggoonurs Green
Keephill Highwell Cottage Pool Hall Burly
The Wells Oldhouse
Birchenfield Little Frome Upper Winslow
Sturts Coopers Green Frome Mill Vicarage Lower house
Halfway House Hackley Goodshop Avenbury Burly Ashmor
Crows Ash Avenbury Court Woolner hill
Newhouse Mintridge Brook House Hyde
Purtush Heath Grove Barnes Birch Hall Stone House
The Heath Ciscop The Grieve
Newton Crick Green Upper Venn
Upper Sollah Hill Oak
Lower Sollah Row Lower Venn
Hall Place Cooke Sedgley Lane Stocks The Rea

Enlarged extract from Ordnance Survey First Edition 1 inch to 1 mile map (Old Series) 1831

Four
Bridle Road, Edwyn Ralph

This green lane at Edwyn Ralph is an example of an ancient route through open fields where its banks are still visible. In the past it may have been enclosed with hedges or fences, but they have been removed long ago. It was known as the Bridle Road in 1841, and has been specially chosen to feature a pack horse trail in this publication. Unfortunately the route of this bridleway through the Black Venn estate was 'stopped up' in January 2010 on the grounds of 'being unnecessary'. A diversion was made around the high banked lake along a recently created bridleway, therefore the old way through Black Venn cannot be investigated and only viewed from aerial photographs on the sale particulars.

The ancient route is rejoined to the east of Black Venn at the brook which is crossed by a pack horse bridge 'constructed of slabs on the surface, similar to a clapper bridge'. It is a narrow and level bridge built of stone for use as a bridle or pack horse bridge, and carries the 'old road' that was known to run from Edwyn Ralph to Black Venn and Saltmarsh. From the bridge the Bridle Road ascends through fields, where some evidence of banks remain between the solitary ruin of Wheelbatch Farm and a disused quarry.

History

Many early routes are difficult to date and identify although some have survived as footpaths, bridleways and byways. At Edwyn Ralph the Bridle Road from Black Venn and past the remaining house and buildings at Wheelbatch led along a route known as an 'old road that runs from Saltmarsh', where the route would have continued to Sandy Cross. From this crossroads a known 'ancient way' led to Whitbourne via a 'now gated road', then joined the road from Bromyard to Worcester 'said to have been a saltway from Droitwich'. These ancient routes radiated from Droitwich in varying directions transporting salt used in the manufacturing of paper, soap, dyes and medicinal products, so 'the importance of its transportation through the centuries has played a large part in the construction of the roadway system'.

50

...County of Worcester, and for making several new lines of road connected therewith in the same Counties in consideration of the sum of Twenty nine Pounds to us paid by John Millechap of the said Town of Bromyard, Boot and Shoe Manufacturer Do hereby grant and release to the said John Millechap All that Cottage or Tenement situate in the Township of Winslow in the Parish of Bromyard in the County of Hereford erected by the Trustees of the said Roads for the purpose of a Toll house at the Turnpike Gate known as "Panniers Lane Gate", together with the Board, Gate, Posts and Appurtenances thereto belonging And al...

Panniers Lane Gate 1875, Bromyard

Panniers Lane tollhouse, Bromyard

As its name suggests the Bridle Road developed as a route for the use of horses and pedestrians, not wide enough for horse drawn vehicles but suitable for transporting goods by packhorses. Before the improvement of roads by the turnpike trusts during the first half of the 18th century, the roads in Herefordshire were 'impassable, impenetrable, churned into mud by horses hooves and deeply rutted by wheeled vehicles' so sure-footed packhorses were a faster and more reliable form of transporting goods than by carts and wagons. A variety of goods including wool, malt, pottery, lead, coal, textiles, salt and even wine were carried on panniers slung across the animals back.

Between Black Venn and Wheelbatch the Bridle Road, marked on an estate map of 1841 and recorded by Herefordshire Council in 1952, crosses a packhorse bridge over a tributary of the river Frome. Packhorse bridges are recognisable for being narrow and having low or no parapets, so that the goods in the loaded panniers were not damaged. This bridge has been identified as a clapper bridge constructed of stone slabs, and possibly dating from the 17th century. Although this is the only bridge that has been listed, it appears that other bridges crossing the Frome and its tributaries on this route also fall into this category.

Black Venn, meaning a dark fen, is a mysterious place known to date from at least the 17th century and mentioned in 1705 as 'Black Fenne' leased 'for three lives for £4 per annum, 1 couple of capons and the best beast on the fall of each life'. From this date the Smith family were associated with Black Venn with Thomas Smith recorded there in 1840 together with Robert Phillips Esq. of Buckenhill Manor owning fields and cottages. The Smiths were still farming at Black Venn in 1867, but since then the 'small farmhouse believed to date back to 1800 has been sympathetically enlarged, developed and transformed by its current owners who have undertaken a comprehensive scheme of improvement and expansion since their purchase over 20 years ago. The result of this venture is a most impressive, inspiring and unique estate offering seclusion in the most beautiful countryside Herefordshire has to offer.'

The old roads and bridle routes from Bromyard, Buckenhill and Edwyn Ralph meeting at Black Venn suggest it was a place of importance in earlier times, and the packhorse style bridges along the route are of significance. Apart from the one at Black Venn, another on route from Brickhouse to Black Venn was described in 1952 as a '6ft wide masonry arch bridge, 10 ft span'. Near New House Farm a tarmac lane leads over another narrow

52

Buckenhill 1856, Saltmarsh

Bridle Road 1841, Edwyn Ralph

Bridle Road

WHEELBATCH . 438

436

437

arched bridge before a green lane leads through Buckenhill Wood to Bromyard Downs, a route clearly marked in 1817 and on the Buckenhill Estate plan of 1856.

On Bromyard Downs the Royal Oak dating from the 18th century was considered to have been a droving inn. About that time Edward Millard was hauling stone from Bromyard Downs and Capler to Hereford to repair the cathedral's collapsed west front. A landlord at the Royal Oak in the mid 19th century was listed as a carrier to Worcester together with two others in Bromyard and Richard Green, a cattle dealer on the Downs. The Royal Oak was shut for a short period but was reopened, and is now the only licensed survivor from several that once existed on the downs, including the Holly Tree which was closed in 2010.

In Bromyard the name 'Panniers Lane' may have derived from the panniers carried by the packhorses. Panniers Lane was named in the sale particulars of Northfield Farm and Flaggoners Green in 1872, and in 1885 when the 'Toll house at the Turnpike Gate known as Panniers Lane Gate together with the Garden, Gate, Posts and appurtenances' were sold by the turnpike trustees for £29. The inns and beer houses in the town would have served the traders and travellers especially the Bay Horse, a name associated with packhorses, which from 1802 was run by the Devereux family.

Exploring Bridle Road

Bromyard is a small market town in the north-east of Herefordshire where the river Frome skirts the eastern edge of the town. The church of St. Peter's, dating from Saxon times, stands in a prominent position in Church Lane which leads directly down to the Frome crossed by a pack horse bridge. Footpaths and bridleways lead to Edwyn Ralph through the river valley where further bridges cross the tributaries of the Frome. Buckenhill Manor and Black Venn are easily identifiable before crossing a bridge identified by archaeologists as a 'clapper bridge' leading up the Bridle Road of 1841 to the ruins of Wheelbatch. The route continues along a tarmac lane and a green lane through Buckenhill Wood leading to Bromyard Downs. A superb stretch across the open downs leads to the outskirts of Bromyard.

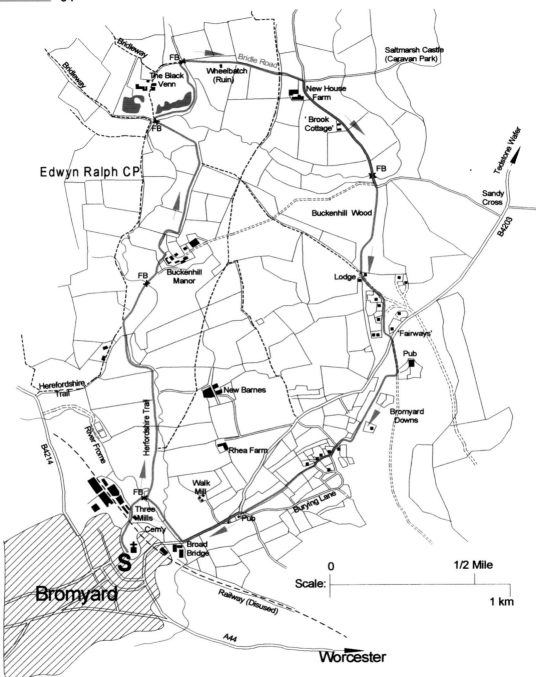

Bridleway

Bridleway

Bridle Road

FB

Saltmarsh Castle
(Caravan Park)

The Black
Venn

Wheelbatch
(Ruin)

New House
Farm

'Brook
Cottage'

FB

Edwyn Ralph CP

FB

Buckenhill Wood

Tedstone Water

Sandy
Cross

B4203

FB

Buckenhill
Manor

Lodge

'Fairways'

Pub

Herefordshire
Trail

New Barnes

Bromyard
Downs

Herefordshire Trail

River Frome

B4214

Rhea Farm

Walk
Mill

Buying Lane

FB

Three
Mills

Pub

Cemy

Broad
Bridge

0   1/2 Mile

Scale:

1 km

Bromyard

Railway (Disused)

A44

Worcester

Length	7 miles OS Map Explorer 202
Start	St Peter's Church, Bromyard GR 6555548
Parking	Car park in Church Lane, Bromyard
Refreshments	Cafes and pubs in Bromyard plus
	Royal Oak Inn (01885 482585), Bromyard Downs
Public Transport	Various bus services to Bromyard

Circular Route

From St. Peter's Church walk down Church Lane and cross the former railway track to the house at Three Mills where a stile marked as the Herefordshire Trail directs the way. Cross the pack horse bridge and continue through the fields and over stiles in a northerly direction. As the large buildings of Buckenhill Manor come into sight on the right, leave the Herefordshire Trail and bear right along the bridleway towards the manor.

Another arched bridge is crossed and a short length of green lane is followed to a gate on the left where the bridleway skirts the stone walls of Buckenhill Manor and continues ahead to an arched bridle bridge at Black Venn. In 2010 the bridleway was officially diverted around the southern edge of the lake to a point where it turns east across a pack horse bridge. The way ahead leads along the Bridle Road and past the stark ruins of Wheelbatch and ascends to the road opposite the gatehouse to Saltmarsh Castle.

The tarmac lane leads south to Buckenhill Wood where a signed footpath along a partly sunken green lane ascends to the lodge on the drive to Buckenhill Manor. The right of way follows the drive past the lodge and onto the northwest portion of Bromyard Downs. From a property called West View cross the common to Fairways, a stone cottage overlooking the B road from Bromyard to Tedstone Wafer.

Carefully cross this busy road and follow the signed tarmac lane to Bromyard Downs and the Royal Oak Inn. Opposite the pub turn right onto the downs, and shortly left along the wide remains of a former race track for a few hundred yards. Reluctantly leave the wide swath of grass and follow a sunken lane to Yew Tree Cottage where a narrow footpath heads through a gate and across meadows towards Bromyard. At the road, pass the Holly Tree Inn (closed at time of writing) and walk along the raised pavement until reaching a signed footpath on the opposite side of the road. This leads through fields back over the pack horse bridge to Three Mills and Church Lane.

Pack Horse Bridge, Black Venn, Edwyn Ralph

Pack Horse Bridge, Bromyard

Sources

Books
- *Hereford Ramblers Association, Herefordshire Trail 2004*
- *B Smith, Herefordshire Maps 2004*
- *P Williams, Whitbourne 1979*
- *J Hillaby & E Pearson eds., Bromyard 1987*
- *P Hindle, Roads and Tracks 2001*
- *J Webb, Memorials of the Civic War 1879*
- *D Gerhold, Carriers & Coachmasters 2005*
- *J Eisel & R Shoesmith, The Pubs of Bromyard and Ledbury 2003*
- *Herefordshire Directories 1858, 1867*
- *H Hurley ed. Landscape Origins of the Wye Valley 2008*
- *Visit Bromyard c2009*

Archives
- *Herefordshire Council Order 2010*
- *Saltmarsh Castle Estate sale 1841 HRO B54/1*
- *Sale of Panniers Toll House 1885 HRO Q/CE/1*
- *Sale of Northfield Farm 1872 Bromyard History Society A66/4*
- *Photograph of Panniers Toll House Bromyard History Society P4*
- *Edwyn Ralph ROW 1952, HRO CD31/2*
- *Norton ROW 1952, HRO CD31/3*
- *Buckenhill Estate plan 1856 HRO C97/3*
- *John Leech's vouchers 1789, HCA 5715/3/1-82*

Journals and Newsletters
- *TWNFC 1921*
- *Bromyard & District Local History Society Newsletter 1971*

Maps
- *Edwyn Ralph and Bromyard Tithe Maps 1841, 1844; Bryant 1835; Price 1817*

Websites
- *Herefordshire Sites and Monuments www.smr.herefordshire.gov.uk*
- *Kyre Park Charters www.archive.org/…/kyreparkcharters00amphuoft*
- *Strutt and Parker www.struttandparker.com*
- *Archenfield Archaeology www.archenfield.com*
- *Cotswold History www.cotswolds.info/cotswolds-heritage.shtml 5*

Lower Townend

Mayfields

Moorfields

Sugar Croft

Bush Farm

Coddington

Pound

Grange Farm

Coomb Hill

Moor Croft Farm

Coddington Farm

Pit house

Marjorum

Worfields

Old Colwall

Southfield

Bra

Raycomb Wood

Sparrow Hill

Priors Court

Peos Farm

Canon heath Wood

Rattal Wood

Cummins Farm

Upper House

Lockster Greens

Hope End

The Farm

Old Turnpike

Withers Farm

Wellington Heath

Stonehouse

es Brook

Dogberry Pools

Petty France

Le Burtons

Frith

Root Farm

Frith Farm

Wood

Massingte Fa

Hill Top

Upper Mitchell

Winsters Elms Copse

Bradlow

Kilbury Camp

Lower Mitchell

Beggars Ash

Hill

Sitch Wood

New Mill

T.P.

Dog Hill

White House

Kidde Way

Wall Farm

Eastnor Hill

Somers Arms

Lodge

LEDBURY

Upper Hall

E

ree rm

T.P.

T.P.

Eastnor

Wood

Eastnor P

Keeper

Enlarged extract from Ordnance Survey First Edition 1 inch to 1 mile map (Old Series) 1831

Five

Green Lane, Dog Hill, Ledbury

From the Market House in the centre of Ledbury, Church Street leads to the start of Green Lane, which is accessed by a shallow flight of steps. A Ledbury Civic Trust plaque confirms 'Green Lane Old Packhorse Road to Worcester' which steeply ascends as a stony track to Dog Hill Wood. Where it divides, the Green Lane continues in a northerly direction as a broad track along the outskirts of the wood. Tumbling stone walls overgrown with ivy will be noticed, all that remains of buildings that once belonged to the Upper Hall estate.

Although traditionally known as a packhorse road of ancient origin, this green lane does not have any features associated with such routes. It has obviously been widened and levelled over the centuries for the use of horse drawn-vehicles and droves of livestock heading for Ledbury market. In 1919 the Upper Hall estate was sold to the Herefordshire County Council, including Dog Hill Wood which is now maintained by the town council together with a network of paths across the wooded hill. In springtime the lane is bordered with a variety of wild flowers and in autumn the foliage of the semi-natural woodland provides a colourful sight.

History

Church Street formed part of an early route to Worcester, but when it was replaced by a new road to Worcester the street lost its importance and became known as Back Lane. During the Middle Ages it was also known as Hallend due to passing both Lower and Upper Halls. When a main thoroughfare, the street would have been busy with traders, and lined with inns offering rest and refreshment to weary travellers. In 1701 'All that Messuage house or Tenement known by the sign of the Fish….situate and lying in a Street called the Back Lane' changed hands. Other inns recorded include the former White Hart and the surviving Prince of Wales.

In 1721 the first Turnpike Road Act in Herefordshire was passed for 'Repairing the several Roads leading from the Town of Ledbury.' The most significant improvement was replacing the ancient road along Church Street

Georgii Regis.

An Act for Repairing the several Roads leading from the Town of *Ledbury* in the County of *Hereford*, to the several Places therein mentioned.

Whereas the several Highways or Roads leading from the Borough and Town of Ledbury in the County of Hereford, to the Parish of Bromsborough in the County of Gloucester, being Three Miles, or thereabouts, and to a Place called the Rye Meadow, in the Parish of Muchmarcle in the said County of Hereford, being Four Miles, or thereabouts, and to a Place called the Broad Field in the Parish of Aylton in the said County of Hereford, &c.

Ledbury Road Act 1721

Sale of the Fish Inn 1701, Ledbury

the yeare of our Lord God according to the computation [...] ward Jones of the Towne of Ledbury in the county of [...] for and in consideracon of the Sume of Forty Poun[...] unto the said Edward Jones the Father at or before th[...] doth hereby acknowledge And thereof and of every par[...] nts his heires Execu[to]rs and Adm[inistrato]rs And also for and in consideraco[...] said Some And for other causes and valluable consideracons hi[...] and confirmed And by these p[re]sents doth grant bargaine & [...] house or tenement knowen by the Sign of the Fish wherein [...] to of and from Thomas Bullocke and by him heretofore of Joh[...] foresaid extending from the said Streete on the South part v[...] t and Lands of them the said Frances Wild and Elizabeth Wild [...] Comodityes profitts priviledges hereditaments and apptin[...] [...] to the same respectively All which said tenements [...]

and Green Lane with a new route to Malvern and Worcester along Horse Lane providing an easier gradient for horse-drawn vehicles. The tolls collected went towards maintaining and improving the roads, but this system was unpopular in Ledbury where serious riots were recorded. In 1735 the rioters 'assembling themselves in a Body of about 200, proceeded to cut down the six several Turnpikes' which surrounded the town. Only two prisoners were taken but others were warned they would be 'brought to Justice'.

In the late 18th century two lanes once led north from Upper Hall and the churchyard to join the Worcester road, one was described as a 'private road' and the other as Hellpitt Lane which was 'stopped up' during the Inclosures of 1813. Due to this the Green Lane may have seen more use by local traffic going to Bradlow and Colwall, as by 1831 it is boldly named on a map as 'Green Lane' following the eastern boundary of Dog Hill Wood.

The Ledbury Guide of 1831 encouraged tourists and residents to visit Dog Hill within a five minute walk to view, 'an abrupt picturesque eminence, overlooking a country of most unequalled luxuriance and fertility. The orchards of Herefordshire are here spread before us in their famed profusion, powerfully striking us with ideas of plenty and munificence'. The writer continues in this style ending with 'Lines Written on Dog Hill'. All this promotion suggests that the Green Lane and Dog Hill Wood had become a pleasant amenity to the town.

The turnpike trustees improved and realigned the roads and moved toll houses to catch the maximum number of road users. By 1835 a toll house was situated at the northern end of the Green Lane where Knapp Lane joins Cut Throat Lane at Bradlow. The toll house was known locally as the Box of Dominoes, and although the roads had been de-tolled it was still standing in 1919 when the Upper Hall estate was sold. The sale particulars described it as 'The Cottage and Garden known as The Old Turnpike', and Dog Hill Wood was advertised as a 'Woodland containing a valuable lot of Oak and Elm, chiefly Oak ripe for cutting'. The whole estate was purchased by Herefordshire County Council who must have demolished the old toll house.

From Bradlow remnants of a green lane leads steeply up to Bradlow Knoll otherwise known as Gallow Hill, where in 1831 you were 'admitted to a prospect the most delightful and comprehensive' probably not aware that Edward Farr of Eastnor was hanged here for the murder of Jane Badland in 1583. The path continues as a ridgeway to Hope End in Coddington where only the coach and stables remain of the home associated with Elizabeth Barrett-Browning. From 1826 the parish roads of Coddington were improved 'about 1500 tons of

Ledbury 1850

Ledbury Riot 1735

We hear from Ledbury in Herefordshire, that a great Riot happen'd there on Saturday Night, the 20th of this Instant, on Account of the Turnpikes, which about three Weeks ago were new erected round that Town. The Commissioners were in Hopes, that the Act passed last Sessions of Parliament, which makes the cutting down of Turnpikes Felony without Benefit of Clergy, would have deterred all Persons from attempting any Thing of that sort again. But it being publickly and currently reported for several Days before, that there would be an armed Gang (as there was in June 1734,) who were resolved that Night, at all Adventures, to demolish them a second Time; some of the Commissioners in and near Ledbury, mustering up what Strength they could, determined to give them a Meeting, with a Design to oppose Force with Force, in case there should be Occasion. Accordingly these Gentlemen, between Seven and Eight in the Evening, marched with their Attendants well armed through the Town, towards the Home-End Turnpike, which leads towards Hereford.

They write from Herefordshire, that the Turnpike Cutters having often threatned to set their Fellow Rioters at Liberty, it was expected every Hour, that they would have attempted Hereford Goal; but the Keeper had provided himself a Quantity of Arms for his Defence: Whereupon they sought an Opportunity to be reveng'd of him; and accordingly, he being at Ross-Fair on Monday Se'nnight, was met at the King's-Head-Inn by more than twenty of the Turnpike-Levellers, who ask'd his Name, and if he did not keep the County-Goal, and for what Reasons he kept two Men in Custody belonging to their Society: The Goaler had not Time to give them an Answer, but was dragg'd immediately out of the House into the Street, there knock'd down, and almost murdered, notwithstanding all possible Endeavours of the Landlord and his Servants to prevent them, who were all barbarously used. They took him afterwards to a Place called Wilton's-Bridge, where they concluded to throw him into the River Wye; but a Confusion arising amongst them how they should dispose of him, it was afterwards agreed to carry him stone was raised broken and laid, drains and culverts made, and over 200 yards of quickset hedges planted' costing just under £87. This probably included the lane passing the church now defined as a footpath along a well defined green lane before proceeding across the Coddington Vineyard – containing 3,000 vines that produce about 3,000 bottles of wine a year.

Field paths from Coddington lead to Raycomb Lane, known as Raycomb Wood Lane in 1835. This route joined Dogberry Lane, now Church Lane, at Wellington Heath. The scattered settlement of old and new houses and cottages is linked by a network of lanes and paths. During the 18th century it had been possible to 'establish a squatters right on a common' provided a house could be marked out, a hearth built, a fire lit and a pot put on to boil before the commoners discovered it and evicted the squatter'. A remaining example of a squatters cottage which had been listed as a grade II building was sold in 2009.

Under the terms of an Enclosure Act the common land was enclosed and roads were laid out at Wellington Heath between 1813 and 1816. At Ochre Hill a wide and level lane leads down to the Pub Lane of that period, where the Farmer's Arms has survived from its origins as New House in 1851. From a small communal garden called the Pool Piece, outside the pub, a footpath gradually ascends to the western outskirts of Frith Wood, where traces of a holloway marked on earlier maps may be identified before returning to Ledbury.

Exploring Green Lane, Dog Hill, Ledbury

This splendid hilly route starts from the market town of Ledbury, but instead of following Church Lane, one of the prettiest cobbled lanes in Herefordshire, take the more direct road signed Church Street to Dog Hill and its Green Lane. From Bradlow a steep path leads up to Bradlow Knoll and enters the delights of Frith Wood where mounds, ditches and boundary banks have been identified. On reaching Hope End another climb ascends Oyster Hill before reaching the tiny village of Coddington. From the church green lanes and field paths lead to and through a vineyard to Raycomb Lane leading to Wellington Heath and Ochre Hill where sections of old ways return to Ledbury.

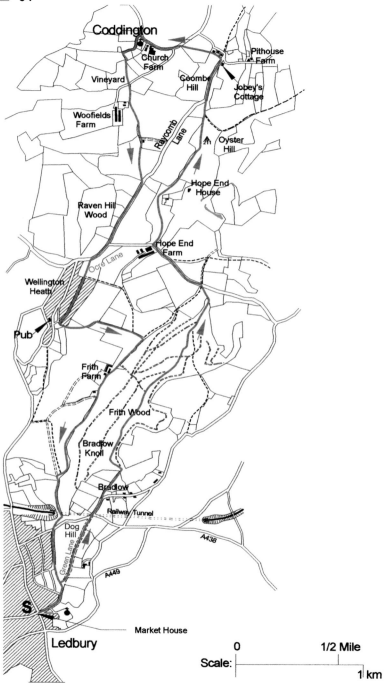

Coddington

Church
Farm

Pithouse
Farm

Vineyard

Coombe
Hill

Jobey's
Cottage

Woofields
Farm

Raycomb Lane

Oyster
Hill

Hope End
House

Raven Hill
Wood

Hope End
Farm

Ocre Lane

Wellington
Heath

Pub

Frith
Farm

Frith Wood

Bradlow
Knoll

Bradlow

Railway Tunnel

Dog
Hill

A438

Green Lane

A449

S

Market House

Ledbury

Scale:

0

1/2 Mile

1 km

Length	**9 miles OS Map Explorer 190**
Start	**Market House GR712377 in Ledbury centre**
Parking	**Town centre car parks**
Refreshments	**Tearooms, cafés, pubs in Ledbury, Farmer's Arms**
	(01531 632010), Wellington Heath
Public Transport	**Buses and trains into Ledbury**

Circular Route

From the Market House in Ledbury follow Church Street past its surviving pub and around a bend to shallow steps leading up to Dog Hill. Within a few hundred yards bear right along Green Lane which widens before reaching Bradlow and Cut Throat Lane. The road ahead leads to a cottage on the left, where a signed path leads steeply up to Bradlow Knoll and into Frith Wood with its wonderful array of spring flowers, chestnut coppices and far reaching views seen between the trees.

At the northern end of Frith Wood a road is followed left to Hope End where a signed path on the right leads through the estate to Oyster Hill, passes a trig point and descends to Coombe Hill. Almost opposite the attractively named Jobey's Cottage follow a field path to Coddington, where a road from a junction leads into the village with its secluded church.

From the opposite side of the graveyard follow the signs leading along a lane and do not miss a hidden stile on the left leading through Coddington Vineyard, with its attractive buildings and well tended vines. The footpath continues across a farm road, and proceeds across stiles and through fields to the left of Woofields Farm and ascends to Raycomb Lane.

This tarmac lane leads to Wellington Heath, but before reaching the rows of houses and cottages turn left at Swallow Stables. The footpath soon reaches Ochre Hill with a wide unmade track which ends as a typical green lane opposite the village pub. If not visiting the hostelry turn sharply left along an unsurfaced lane leading to a field path. A footbridge crosses a brook before an ascent is made through the fruit growing fields of Frith Farm.

A stile leads into the western boundary of the wood where sections of an old lane can be identified. The route passes Frith Farm, its orchards, disused quarries and a permissive footpath leading into Frith Wood managed by the Forestry Commission. Their information board may be studied before continuing along the wide track which crosses the railway tunnel at Bradlow. A little way ahead cross the road and walk through the east side of Dog Hill Wood and return to Ledbury down Church Street.

Green Lane, Dog Hill, Ledbury 2009

Frith Wood, Ledbury

Sources

Books

- *P Garnett, Portrait of Wellington Heath 2002*
- *P Garnett, Upper Hall 1991*
- *P Garnett, Ledbury Alleyways and Yards 1993*
- *J Eisel, R Shoesmith, The Pubs of Bromyard and Ledbury 2003*
- *J Cooper, ed, Ledbury Street Names 2007*
- *L Tilley, Ledbury 1981*
- *J Hillaby, The Book of Ledbury 1982*
- *S Clegg, Exploring Frith Wood 2008*

Archives

- *Ledbury Road Act 1721 HCL*
- *Scrapbook of cuttings HCL*
- *Upper Hall sale particulars 1919, HRO D96/97*
- *Fish Inn deed 1701 HRO L84/9-13*
- *Ledbury Guide 1831, HRO J97/1*

Maps

- *Ledbury map c1780, HCA 7004/1*
- *Ledbury TM 1837*
- *Ledbury Inclosure map 1813*
- *Colwall TM 1842*
- *Coddington TM 1838*
- *Bryant 1835*
- *Price 1817*
- *OS 1831, 2006*

Linburies
Joans hill
Sharpnage Well
Sharpnage Wood
Welchestor
Broadmore Common
Hill House
Rudge Wood
Rudge End
Westington
Hill
Mabley Grove
Lea Wood
Fishpool Hill
Paget's Wood
Buckley
Low.r Buckenhill
Oldbury
Iva Ho.s
Capler Farm
Buckenhill
Gore Farm
Camp
New Tithing
Dockwell Farm
Shop Farm

Park Farm
Canwood
Woodcott
Wood House
Little Canwood
Nardens
Devereux Park
Wood
Bent.t Orchards
Nardens
Overbury
Scar
Woolhope
Winslow Hill
Green Hill
Beans Bat
Beans Batt Wood
The Court
Poundfield
Black House
Hollinghill
Stoney Hill
Fowners
Holling Hill Wood
Twittis
Little Burland
Crews
Sleaves Oak
Hyde
Yager
Sapnells
Marcle Hill
Whittlebury Wood
Court
Sollers Hope
Whittlebury
Histen
Lindels
Knap
Fisholes
The Pound
Camp
Eaton

Enlarged extract from Ordnance Survey First Edition 1 inch to 1 mile map (Old Series) 1831

6

Lindells Lane, Sollers Hope

Lindells Lane leads from a place called Firs Cross on Marcle Ridge to Sollers Hope a distance of '1.025 miles' as measured by Herefordshire Council in 1936. Although leading from the ancient ridgeway the lane probably developed at a later period as its width, deepness and partly stoned surface suggests. Its zigzag course probably developed as a route used by horse-drawn vehicles which required gradual gradients. With its stoned surface the lane survives as a good example of a typical 18th century road. In fact it is an unclassified road open to all vehicles, which includes walkers, riders, cyclists, horse-drawn vehicles and motorised traffic.

From Marcle Ridge the lane is broad and narrows as it descends and winds down between banks and hedges to Grey Hill Barn, a converted barn, where a particularly wet section has been covered with rubble. On the left-hand side is a hilly meadow known in the mid 19th century as Lime Kiln Bank, and below Lyndalls Wood on the edge of the lane is a lime kiln with draw holes below and an overgrown charging hole above dating from the time that this lane was used as a limestone way. The remainder of Lindells Lane serves as a road with access to Lindalls farm and other properties in Sollers Hope.

History

The parishes of Sollers Hope, Woolhope and Fownhope lie on the limestone hills which form the Woolhope Dome where the quarrying and burning of limestone became an important industry. Over the centuries lime has been in demand for tanning, building, agriculture and medicinal products. The earliest known records of quarrying stone in this area dates from 1585 at Buckenhill for 'tenants getting and selling stone' and in 1697 for 'the right to mine for coals' in Woolhope, Fownhope and Sollers Hope. In 1698 payments were made for carrying stone and filling a kiln at Harris's Hill and in 1777 'as much Lime as can be bought for five Pounds at the Lime Kilns in the Parish of Fownhope' was ordered for a farm at Madley.

Once the limestone had been cut from the nearby quarries, the lime burner's job was to place layers of limestone and fuel into the charge hole at the top of

I have obliged my self to find Lime to dress all the Arable Land once over which is 124 Acres, I am to allow a Dozen Barrels for each acre which at ten shillings a Dozen comes to 62:12:00. I could not set the Farm to any Person that was able to pay the rent of it upon Better Terms. As to the Great Tithes they are now set for 82:07:03 Out of which I pay to seven Prebends 08:00:00 a piece and Six Pounds to the Vicar which amount to 62:00:0 'Twas Customary to provide a Dinner at the Alehouse for those that came to pay their tithe. There was allways allow'd 03:10:00 for it but I have entertain'd them at my own house which has not lessen'd the Expence. one year with another I have not receiv'd 80:00:0 which is paid in small sums at

Lime for Court Farm 1728, Woolhope

Lindells Lane limekilns and 1794 & 1824 advertisements

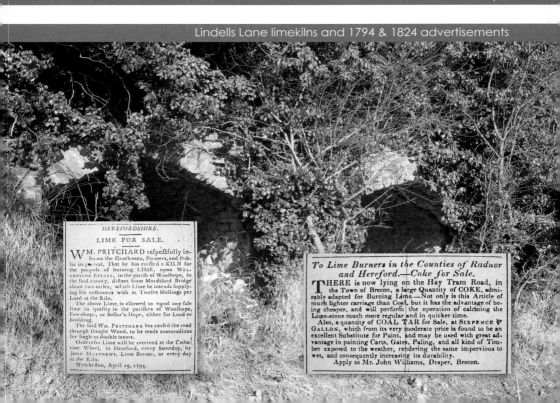

HEREFORDSHIRE.

LIME FOR SALE.

WM. PRITCHARD respectfully informs the Gentlemen, Farmers, and Public in general, That he has erected a KILN for the purpose of burning LIME, upon WELCHESTON ESTATE, in the parish of Woolhope, in the said county, distant from Mordiford Bridge about two miles; which Lime he intends supplying his customers with at, Twelve Shillings per Load at the Kiln.

The above Lime, is allowed to equal any sale lime in quality in the parishes of Woolhope, Fownhope, or Sollar's-Hope, either for Land or Building.

The said WM. PRITCHARD has caused the road through Haught Wood, to be made commodious for single or double teams.

Orders for Lime will be received at the Catherine Wheel, in Hereford, every Saturday, by JOHN MATTHEWS, Lime Burner, or every day at the Kiln.

Welcheston, April 29, 1794.

To Lime Burners in the Counties of Radnor and Hereford.—Coke for Sale.

THERE is now lying on the Hay Tram Road, in the Town of Brecon, a large Quantity of COKE, admirably adapted for Burning Lime.—Not only is this Article of much lighter carriage than Coal, but it has the advantage of being cheaper, and will perform the operation of calcining the Lime-stone much more regular and in quicker time.

Also, a quantity of COAL TAR for Sale, at SIXPENCE P GALLON, which from its very moderate price is found to be an excellent Substitute for Paint, and may be used with great advantage in painting Carts, Gates, Paling, and all kind of Timber exposed to the weather, rendering the same impervious to wet, and consequently increasing its durability.

Apply to Mr. John Williams, Draper, Brecon.

the kiln, and fire the furnace from below. This produced clinker which fell into the draw hole at the bottom and if slated with water produced a fine powder of lime. This product was in demand from the late 18th century for agricultural improvement. William Prichard of Woolhope was supplying 'lime in quality' at 'Twelve Shillings per Load' in 1794, and improved a road from Woolhope to Mordiford 'for single and double teams' to transport the lime down to the Wye. The 1796 account of an unnamed kiln in the area shows the costs of burning, riddling, price of baskets and powder, labour of smith and carpenter, and '238 dozen Coal', '1 load Stone' and rent for one year, which totalled £164 0s 8 ½ d for producing '559 doz. Lime'.

John Morris occupied Lindalls farm with its lime workings for several decades from the late 18th century, and evidence of his trade has been found in the barge accounts. There are records of 'loads' and 'baskets' of lime coal being freighted on barges along the Wye for Mr. Morris, Mr. Hill and the Winniatt family of Woolhope and Sollers Hope. Although lime was still being conveyed by barge in 1824, the trade began to decline when the large scale Radnorshire Lime Works were established, which eventually superseded the local lime industry. In 1839 'Lyndale Homestead & yard' and the surrounding farmland was owned by Thomas Price and occupied by John Brown in 1857.

The Woolhope Naturalist's Field Club in August 1868 'made its annual visit to the district from which it takes its name' and the first place visited was the 'Lindels limestone quarry' where members with hammers collected and examined fossils. From the quarry the party in 'two well-laden coaches' followed the lane to the ridge and the 'Camp on Oldbury Hill'. Having enjoyed the 'magnificent and almost panoramic' views the party continued to the quarry at Sleaves Oak, now the Ridge Hill picnic site.

The Club made no reference to the former lime industry, as the members were only interested in the geological formation of the landscape and examining the exposed rocks for fossils. From Hooper's Oak they returned through Woolhope village then made a rapid descent down the road that had been improved by William Prichard, which took them past 'Littlehope or Scutterdine quarries which could only be glanced at' before reaching the turnpike road at Mordiford. Another paper on geology was published in the transactions of 1902 describing Lindels or Lindalls Quarries 'with many fossils' that were lying '1 mile E from Sollers Hope, ½ mile W from Oldbury Camp'.

Between Sollers Hope church and Lower Buckenhill, field paths meet at a place called New Gore, where the path followed to the north appears to be a continuation of an old hollow-way traditionally known as the Pilgrims Way. It

Lime burners in 1803

Lindells Lane 2009, Sollers Hope

passes a site believed to be the lost chapel of St Dyfrig who founded a chapel or shrine in Woolhope. In 1514 it was in need of attention when Bishop Mayhew granted indulgences for contributions to 'the support of the shrine (sacellum) of the Trinity at Woolhope (Hope Wolwith), commonly called S. Dubricius'. A piscine found in 1954 led to an excavation two years later in a field near Lower Buckenhill Farm, but only stones below the surface were discovered.

One other lane at Woolhope is worthy of mention, leading beyond The Court from the Butcher's Arms Inn. This lane known as Butcher's Arms Lane in 1952 is an unclassified road until reaching the open fields on Harris's Hill where it continues as a footpath to Hooper's Oak. The lime kilns and quarries on this hill were worked by the Winniatt family who were recorded at Court Farm in 1728 when the Dean and Chapter property was 'in a very bad condition'. A 'new farm house' was built and its 'outhouses' were repaired for a total of £150 before being leased to Richard Winniatt who agreed 'to find lime to dress all the Arable land once over which is 124 acres' and 'to allow a Dozen Barrels for each acre which at ten shillings a dozen comes to £2 12s 0d'. It was also customary for the tenant 'to provide a Dinner at the Alehouse for those that came to pay their tithe'.

The lime for Court Farm would have been carted down Butcher's Arms Lane from Winniatt's kilns on Harris's Hill, and the 1791 barge accounts record that later Winniatts paid for 'coal, some certainly limecole grade' shipped from the Forest of Dean to wharves along the Wye. From these sites the coal would have been hauled up from the Wye to Woolhope and along Butcher's Arms Lane to fire their kilns on the hill.

Exploring Lindells Lane, Sollers Hope

A long and twisting lane leads down to Sollers Hope from the top of Ridge Hill through the delightful countryside of south-east Herefordshire. In 1936 this route was officially known as Lindells Lane named after the neighbouring wood and farm now shown as Lyndalls Wood and Lindalls. Although the lane has all the characteristics of an old route it was used as a limestone way from the early 18th century together with other paths, lanes and roads featured on this walk. The remains of lime kilns, quarries and stoned surfaces are identifiable along the way at Lyndalls in Sollers Hope and at Buckenhill, Siege Wood, and Harris's Hill in Woolhope.

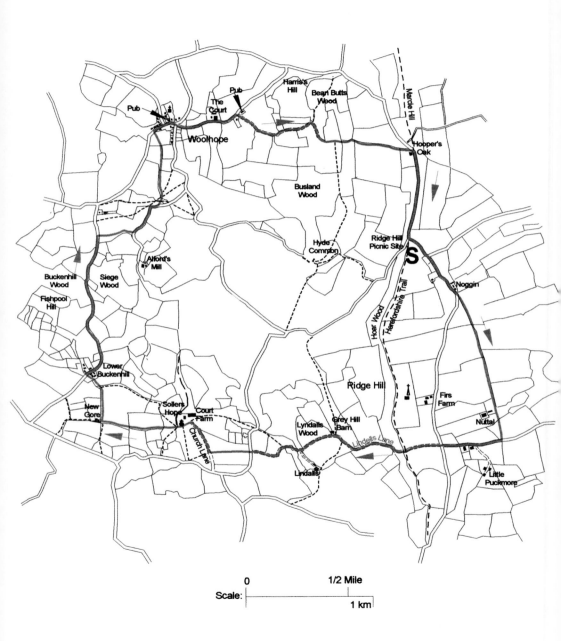

Scale:

0   1/2 Mile

1 km

Length	8 miles
OS Map	Explorer 189
Start	Ridge Hill Picnic Site, 2 miles E Woolhope
Parking	Ridge Hill Picnic Site GR620346
Refreshments	Crown Inn, Woolhope (01432 860468)
	Butcher's Arms Inn, Woolhope (01432 860281)
Public Transport	Not available

Circular Route

From Ridge Hill, with its panoramic views of the Malverns, follow the road leading in a south easterly direction, and after passing Noggin farm follow the signed path which descends over stiles and across fields offering stunning views before reaching a road and Nuttal Cottage. Turn right up the road to a minor crossroads where the start of Lindells Lane lies ahead.

Lindells Lane zigzags down to Grey Hill Barn and Lyndalls Wood where limekilns stand on the edge of the lane opposite a field known in 1839 as Lime Kiln Bank. Further on a road is crossed where a field path leads ahead to Church Lane, leading to Sollers Hope Church. From the idyllically sited church follow the path through the churchyard, cross a footbridge and continue ahead to a junction of paths at New Gore. Take the right hand path down to Lower Buckenhill with its cluster of farms and barns. Follow the road going north passing Fishpool Hill on the left where limekilns can be viewed from the roadside, and Siege Wood on the right where kilns are hidden by overgrowth and not visible from the road. Beyond a securely gated property a signed bridleway leads left to Alford's Mill Lane which is followed to the left around the bends to a signed footpath heading for Woolhope Church with its tower seen ahead.

At Woolhope village follow the road to the Crown Inn. At the junction take the middle choice signed to Putley which descends to the Butcher's Arms, where a right turn is taken beside the inn's garden. This lane gradually climbs between hedges to a gate at Harris's Hill, formerly known as Hawthorn Hill. The lane has lost its hedgerows as it passes limekilns and quarries on the hilltop, but at the next gate ahead it is recognised as a green lane descending through woodland to join a field path up to cottages at Hooper's Oak. A right turn along the ridge returns to the start.

Butcher's Arms Inn, Woolhope

Lindells Lane, Sollers Hope

Sources

Books
- *Herefordshire Directories 1858, 1867*
- *Bishop Mayhew's Registers 1514*
- *H Hurley, ed. Landscape Origins of the Wye Valley 2008*
- *Herefordshire Council Unclassified Roads 1936*
- *V. Morgan, The Lime Kilns in Walford, Ross Civic Society 2000*

Archives
- *Dispute 1585, HCA 5260*
- *Court Farm 1728, HCA 5065/2*
- *Sollers Hope & Woolhope Land Tax 1747-1799, HRO*
- *Articles of Agreement 1697, HRO E12/IV/172/1-18*
- *Barge accounts 1791,1796, 1810 LOWV*
- *Lease 1777, HRO F37/178*
- *Sollers Hope ROW 1952, HRO CD31/38*
- *Woolhope ROW 1952, HRO CD31/34*
- *V Goodbury, History of Limeburning 1992, HRO BH65/1*

Maps
- *Herefordshire Road Map nd*
- *OS 1831, 1888, 2006*
- *Sollers Hope Tithe Map 1839*
- *Woolhope Tithe Map 1839*
- *Bryant 1835*
- *Herefordshire Road Map 1985*

Journals & Newspapers
- *TWNFC 1868, 1902, 1954, 1956*
- *HAN Spring 1995*
- *Her Jnl 1794, 1824,*

Websites
- *Herefordshire Sites and Monuments www.smr.herefordshire.gov.uk*

Enlarged extract from Ordnance Survey First Edition 1 inch to 1 mile map (Old Series) 1831

7

Elm Lane, Hope Mansell

Since 1888, Ordnance Survey maps have shown Elm Lane leading along the eastern boundary of Hope Mansell parish to Newtown. The lane is a delightful woodland track, soft underfoot with some sections revealing earlier paving. A prominent boundary bank and ditch must have delineated the original county boundary between Herefordshire and Gloucestershire along the rippling Bailey Brook, but subsequent boundary changes have tidied up the parish and county boundaries. The eastern edge of the lane is lined with piles of moss covered stones, presumably the remnants of a former stone wall alongside the Lea Bailey Inclosure.

As the level lane skirts through the mixed woods of the Lea Bailey, it is now hard to imagine it was named Elm Lane as unfortunately since the outbreak of Dutch Elm Disease the magnificent elms do not survive into maturity. From the cottages at Newtown the path narrows as it proceeds through conifer plantations to Baileybrook where a more substantial forestry track is met which twists and turns a gradual ascent passing cottages named Lily, Tump and Cherry Tree before reaching the hamlet at Palmers Flat. Apart from the forestry track these small isolated settlements are also served by footpaths leading down to Hope Mansell.

History

Hope Mansell is a sheltered and secluded parish and is 'flanked by high ground on every side except the north, where the long valley eventually opens out beneath the detached hill-mass of Penyard Park'. On its eastern side it borders the Forest of Dean in Gloucestershire and has been closely associated with Lea Bailey, recorded in the 15th century as being a detached part of Newland parish on the Herefordshire border. It was not until 1884 that boundary changes placed a western part of Lea Bailey into the parishes of Hope Mansell and Weston-under-Penyard.

In medieval times this was an area where the king's deer were threatened by wolves, and wild boars were hunted. Other documents

AN

A C T

For Inclosing Lands in the Parish of *Hopemansel*, in the County of *Hereford*.

WHEREAS there are within the Manor and Parish of Preamb *Hopemanfel*, in the County of *Hereford*, certain Commonable and Wafte Lands called the *Purlieu* : And whereas the Right Rev. Father in God *George Ifaac*, by Divine permiffion Lord Bifhop of *Gloucefter*, is Lord of the faid Manor, and *Thomas Nixon*, Efq. is his Leffee of the faid Manor.

And whereas an Act was paffed in the Forty-firft Year of the Reign of his prefent Majefty, entituled " An Act for confolidat- " ing in One Act certain Provifions, ufually inferted in Acts " of Inclofure, and for facilitating the Mode of proving the " feveral Facts ufually required on the Paffing of fuch Acts."

Hope Mansell Inclosure Act 1806

Hope Mansell Inquisition 1281

Randolf de Sandwich himself came to the wood of the abbot of Gloucester of Hope Mansel and received as foresters and verderers and others and legal people of those parts and by their own view understood that there was no damage or harm to the lord king's forest or to his forest of Dean or the men of those parts if the king were to allow the abbot of Gloucester to fell the said wood in quarters over four years and to his benefit because the said wood is old coppice and thicket and less suitable for the deer grazing than wood which is newly grown and that wolfs ['outlaws' or real wolves?] and criminals often come poaching and hang around in the wood on account of its thickness nevertheless each quarter is enclosed in the 'lower haye' for three years so that our deer can come in and out so that if beasts of the men of those parts may enter that wood as the enclosure is ineffective due it not being permanently enclosed and that the said abbot may have the benefit of sale of wood of each quarter to value of 100 shillings.

record the Lea Bailey in a Hope Mansell Glebe Terrier of 1589 'a brooke called the Baylie Brooke on the easte syde', and a Forest of Dean Survey of 1788 refers to 'a spur including the Lea Bailey woods on the Herefordshire boundary'. A Perambulation of the Parish made in 1834 'commenced at the Bailey brook' and followed a 'road leading from the Bailey to Hope Mansel'. It was not until 1835 that the first known reference to Elm Lane appeared on Sopwith's Map, although the route of the lane is partly shown along the county boundary on maps of 1817 and 1824.

Elm Lane leads from Bailey Gate and closely follows the county boundary to Newtown, where one cottage existed in 1787 followed by several others built after 1834. Further north at Baileybrook cottages were established during the late 18th century and at Palmers Flat a small group of cottages were constructed during the early 19th century. From Palmers Flat the lane becomes less obvious as it continues as a footpath down to Hope Mansell.

Other green lanes of interest at Hope Mansell are recorded in the Inclosure Award of 1808, which inclosed the 'waste lands called the Purlieu in the parish of Hope Mansel' after an act of 1806. The Purlieu was an extensive belt of woodland originally called the Abbott's Purlieu when possessed by St. Peter's Abbey in Gloucester. In 1339 there was a path 'between the abbot's wood of Hopemaloysel and the wood of the forest of Dene....leading thence by a path called Meresty'. This could be one of the paths that now leads through the remains of the Purlieu now existing as Little Purlieu, Purlieu Wood and Upper Purlieu.

The Purlieu like the Forest of Dean was 'darke and terrible by reason of crooked and winding wayes, as also the grisly shade therein, that it made the inhabitants more fierce, and bolder to commit robberies'. Not surprising that in 1795 'a reputed highwayman, and noted deerstalker, named William Stallard' lived on the Upper Purlieu above Hope Mansell. His lawlessness, career as a horse-stealer and involvement and instigator of various outrages eventually led him to the gallows in 1800.

From Deep Dean a deeply sunken lane twists and turns through Chestnut Wood and descends in an easterly direction to Hope Mansell. This is obviously a lane of some antiquity and in the Inclosure Award was described as leading from the Danelo Lime Kilns owned by Joseph Rudge. It was recorded as a private carriageway of 14 foot width and 'for the use of the owner and occupier of the lime kilns and for those fetching lime'. It later became known as Kiln Lane in 1936 and since 1952 its entire length has been upgraded to a byway.

82

attended on the part of the Crown.

William Baldwin of Ruardean on the part of the Lord of the Manor.

The boys present were,

Timothy Bennett } of Hopes Ash
Thomas Bennett

Thomas Holmes — Bailey brook

Jonathan Hodges Hope Mansel

George Jones } Sons of Samuel Jones
James Jones } Laborer near y Stawed

Hope Mansell Perambulations 1834

Elm Lane 1835

Map labels:
Elm Lane
THE LEA BAILEY INCLOSURE
Bailey Gate
From Hope Mansell
LINING
Wigwood
PINCARYS TUMP
BLACKWELL MEADS
Hopes Well
HARP CROVE
MORSE
SCULLY CROVE
MITCHEL DEAN MEEND
UE BLUE
TRUE BLU
DRYBROOK
THE MORSE GROUND
F. Mitchel Dean
Stenders Toll Bar
M8 M7

The other green lane recorded in the Inclosure Award is the existing lane that leads below Upper Purlieu Wood to the start of Elm Lane. In 1808 it was a public carriageway and driftway of 30 foot width 'extending into the course of an ancient road across the Purlieu called Broomhill till communicating with Lea Bailey at the east side of the Purlieu'. In 1952 Herefordshire Council reported it as a 'green lane' in bad condition leading from the main road. It was added to the definitive map partly as a footpath but has since been upgraded to a byway.

Hope Mansell is unfortunate that it has lost its inn, shop and school. Its sole inn at Hawthorns was known as the Crown where a Friendly Society held meetings from the 1840s. After a succession of owners it eventually closed around 1970 retaining the name of Old Inn. The bakery and shop of 1902 at Napple has not survived and the school has been converted to a village hall. The Wonky Donkey, formerly the New Inn, at Pontshill has limited opening hours.

Exploring Elm Lane

This is a wonderful and scenic route around the beautiful Hope Mansell valley, which lies in a secluded corner of southwest Herefordshire. It starts from a little known view point near the Gloucestershire boundary above Horn Hill Farm. From this elevated site there is a panoramic view of the whole valley surrounded by woodland with Hope Mansell village situated in the centre. Footpaths and byways traverse green lanes to Lea Bailey and Elm Lane, which skirts the woods of Lea Bailey past the small settlements at Newtown, Baileybrook and Palmers Flat where footpaths lead down, across and steeply up the wooded slopes of the valley to a road at Deep Dean. The road ascends to the start of a deeply sunken green lane which winds down to Hope Mansell with its church and collection of attractive stone farms, houses and cottages which can be admired before climbing the final footpath returning to the view point.

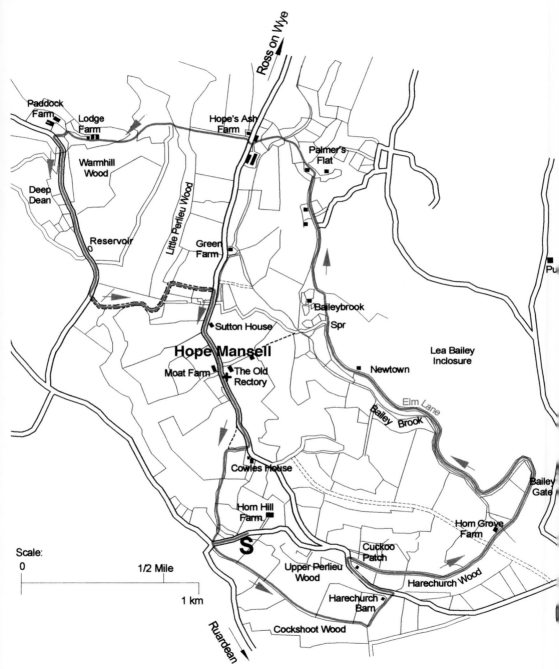

Length	8 miles	OS Map	OL14
Start	Viewpoint at Hope Mansell GR627187 on road above Horn Hill Farm		
Parking	Limited parking at viewpoint		
Refreshments	Bring a picnic		
Public Transport	Not available		

Circular Route

After admiring the scene from the view point walk up the tarmac lane to a road junction and follow the signed path leading south east through fields and over stiles, offering views from the Malverns to the Forest of Dean. The path turns left to pass Harechurch Barn and at the road turn left to an unsurfaced byway starting from behind a cottage called Cuckoo Patch. This green lane leads below Harechurch Wood to Bailey Gate passing Hom Grove Farm with its gushing water spout.

Instead of accessing the road at Bailey Gate keep left within Lea Bailey Inclosure where Elm Lane follows its zigzag boundary alongside the Bailey Brook. The lane winds in a northerly direction through pleasant woodland only interrupted by the tiny settlements at Newtown, Baileybrook and Palmers Flat with its assortment of cottages. At Palmers Flat a narrow footpath descends to Lilac Cottage and a broad track that leads between fields to Hopes Ash Farm and the Hope Mansell road.

Cross the road and walk between the farm buildings where a signed path ascends a field before entering Little Purlieu Wood where a steep climb between large boulders of pudding stone leads to a track at the summit. Waymarks guide the route ahead across a field, down a narrow woodland path to open fields at Lodge Farm in the adjoining parish of Walford, From Lodge Farm the right of way follows the drive to the road at Deep Dean.

Turn left up the road for another ascent, and shortly after passing a grass covered reservoir follow the signed byway leading down to Hope Mansell. In the past this green lane was named Kiln Lane after the lime kilns in the area. It follows a dog leg course which descends to Hope Mansell village. The road is followed past Sutton House and Street Farm with its converted barns and unusual spout of water. A useful village feature is a notice board displaying a map of the footpaths and bridleways of Hope Mansell. Beyond the Old Rectory and the church a sunken footpath on the right is followed into fields where it bears left across stiles to the road junction above the view point.

Lane from Cuckoo Patch, Hope Mansel

Elm Lane boundary bank 2009

Sources

Books

- P. Coones, *The Parish Church of St. Michael 1986*
- *N.M. Herbert, ed. Victoria County History, Gloucestershire Vol V 1996*
- *H. G. Nicholls, Forest of Dean 1858*
- *H. Hurley, The Pubs of Ross and South Herefordshire 2001*
- *Herefordshire Council, Unclassified Roads 1936*

Archives

- *Glebe Terrier 1589 HRO HD2*
- *Perambulation 1834 HRO BO9/1*
- *Inclosure Act 1806 HRO BL52/59*
- *Inclosure Award 1808 HRO Q/RI/20*
- *Patent Roll 1339, printed*
- *Hope Mansell ROW 1952 CD31/36*
- *Inquisition 1281 TNA C143-5*

Maps

- *Sopwith, Forest of Dean 1835*
- *OS 1831, 1888, 2006*
- *1817 Price*
- *Bryant Gloucestershire 1824; Herefordshire 1835*
- *Hope Mansell Tithe Map 1840*
- *Parishes of Herefordshire 1980 HRO*
- *Hope Mansell Definitive Footpath Map 1970s*

Enlarged extract from Ordnance Survey First Edition 1 inch to 1 mile map (Old Series) 1831

8

Rhiw Lane, Longtown

The Rhiw Lane leading from Great Turnant at Llanveynoe was a surprise find on the slopes of the Black Mountains. The section followed is designated on the Ordnance Survey as 'other routes with open access', but officially it is an unclassified road and forms part of a much longer route possibly from Hay to Oldcastle. When explored, the lane was deserted with little evidence of horse's hoof marks and tractor wheel ruts, possibly due to lack of use because of the numerous springs that form boggy patches and rivulets crossed by fords. The lane runs parallel to the more popular ridge walk known as Offa's Dyke which attracts the walkers to follow a higher stretch along the boundary between England and Wales.

This lane from Great Turnant contains most of the features associated with green lanes. The carriageway width is alternatively bordered by moss-covered stone walls, thick hedges or a grassy bank as it leads across the open hillside. Along the section between Turnant and Cwm Farm at least two routes preserved as footpaths lead from the rolling hills of Herefordshire and over the Black Mountains to Llanthony in the Vale of Ewyas. A noticeable feature in this area are the stone stiles which apparently date from at least the 18th century and have proved to have a much longer life than the wooden ones of today.

History

Longtown, Llanveynoe and Clodock were originally in 'an area of Welsh land anciently known as Ewyas, which was claimed by the de Lacy family as overlords'. From the Norman period it became known as Ewyas Lacy a 'frontier country in the Marches of Wales until brought into England and the county of Herefordshire in the 16th century'. Longtown as suggested by its name is a linear village sheltered by the Black Mountains, from which the rivers Olchon and Monnow rise together with numerous brooks. In the past Longtown was a busier place but now only one pub, the school, a village hall and an outdoor education centre serve the

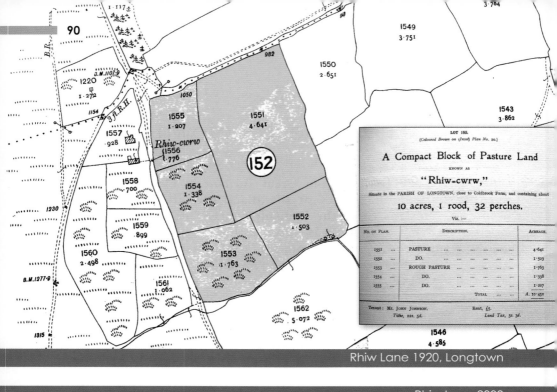

LOT 150.

(Coloured Brown on (Inset) Plan No. 10.)

A Compact Block of Pasture Land

KNOWN AS

"Rhiw-cwrw,"

Situate in the PARISH OF LONGTOWN, close to Coldbrook Farm, and containing about

10 acres, 1 rood, 32 perches.

Viz.:—

No. on Plan.	Description.						Acreage.
1551	...	PASTURE	...	...	...	...	4·641
1552	...	DO.	...	...	...	...	1·503
1553	...	ROUGH PASTURE	...	...	...	...	1·763
1554	...	DO.	...	...	...	...	1·338
1555	...	DO.	...	...	...	...	1·207
					TOTAL	...	A. 10·452

Tenant: Mr. JOHN JOHNSON,   Rent, £5.
Tithe, 12s. 5d.   Land Tax, 3s. 3d.

Rhiw Lane 1920, Longtown

Rhiw Lane 2009

community which has a thriving local historical society. The most notable building in the village is Longtown castle with its ruined remains of a 13th century round keep and curtain walls.

After fording the Olchon and bridging the brooks through the meadows, the footpath leads to Turnant and the green lane known as Rhiw or the Mountain Road, which in 1935 was described as a seven mile route from Pant Farm to Blaen Olchon. In 1803 Great and Little Turnant were occupied by James Nicholls and by 1919 James Williams was farming Upper Turnant, when it was advertised for sale as a 'Valuable and Improvable Farm, consisting of a dwelling-house, Farm Buildings including cart stable for three horses', other outbuildings, a 'Valuable Sheep-Walk' and a total of 94 acres bordering the green lane.

At Rhiw Arw the lane crosses a stretch of open hillside on the boundary of Llanveynoe and Longtown where in 1878 'Bryn Rhiw and Rhiw Cwrw otherwise Troedyrhiw' with 110 acres was in the possession of the Rev. Eagles and offered for sale. It was described as being well watered, on a good road with a right of pasturing 400 sheep on the adjoining mountain. Then in 1920 the Marquess of Abergavenny sold his 2,670 acre Herefordshire estate which included 10 acres at Rhiw-cwrw lying opposite an enclosure of fields known in the 1840s as Cae Rhiw.

Today's name Rhiw Awr means 'ale track' and is derived from the earlier Rhiw-cwrw, a path that crossed the Black Mountains to Llanthony and was recorded in the 8th century in the bounds of Clodock. The 'ale track' has become a fashionable name used in walking guides in the Black Mountains, and from Llanthony Priory 'down the ancient track known as the Beer Trail, monks allegedly transported beer from Longtown to Llanthony'. According to George Borrow in 1862 'cwrw da' was a request for good beer regarded by Archdeacon Coxe in 1801 as the 'national liquor'.

The mountainside at Rhiw Awr is associated with a legendry tale about a man returning from Llanthony to Longtown 'when a fog came on suddenly, and he lost his way. He was standing, quite at loss, when a man came towards him, wearing a large, broad-brimmed hat and a cloak. He did not speak but beckoned, and the man followed him, until he found himself on the right path. Turning round, he thanked his unknown friend, but received no reply: he vanished quickly in the fog'. He later discovered that this man had been dead for two years!

Stile at Clodock

Rhiw awr the 'Beer Trail'

From the Rhiw Awr crossing, the green lane continues past abandoned farms and barns and over a series of fords before a footpath heads east and joins a sunken lane to Cwm, inhabited by William Watkins in 1824, and Cwmcoched mentioned in a survey of Ewyas Lacy in 1705. The Monnow is followed as it flows past the Cornwall Arms and the church at Clodock, which has stood on the same site since around 500 AD. Within the church are some interesting features including an inscribed stone slab attributed to the 9th century. An excellent coloured church guide leads the visitor around the building. A toilet is available and a welcoming touch is an invitation to help yourself to tea or coffee.

The path along the Monnow leads to Upper Pont-hendre where a bridge crosses the Olchon, before returning to Longtown with its solitary pub offering a refreshing break. The Crown dating from 1751 is one of the earliest established pubs in Longtown and is the only survivor from a list of previous licensed houses. There was the Anchor of 1830 at Upper Pont-hendre, the Black Lion of 1867, the Greyhound of 1841 which closed in the 1980s, the New Inn of 1797 now re-used as the Outdoor Education Centre, the Sun of 1818 and the 'Heart a Public House with Garden, large barn, stable etc.' in 1804.

Exploring Rhiw Lane

A wonderful walk from Longtown to discover a little known green lane known as Rhiw or the Mountain Road on the slopes of the Black Mountains. A gradual climb through lush meadows and over swift flowing fords leads to Great Turnant in Llanveynoe where a tarmac lane leads to the start of this green lane leading south towards Oldcastle. The lane associated with legendry tales is followed for at least two miles offering stunning views of the patchwork fields of Herefordshire to the east and the bracken-clad slopes of the Black Darren and Hatterrall Hill rising to the west. A descent is made through fields and along further lanes to the pretty church at Clodock where a riverside path follows the Monnow to Longtown.

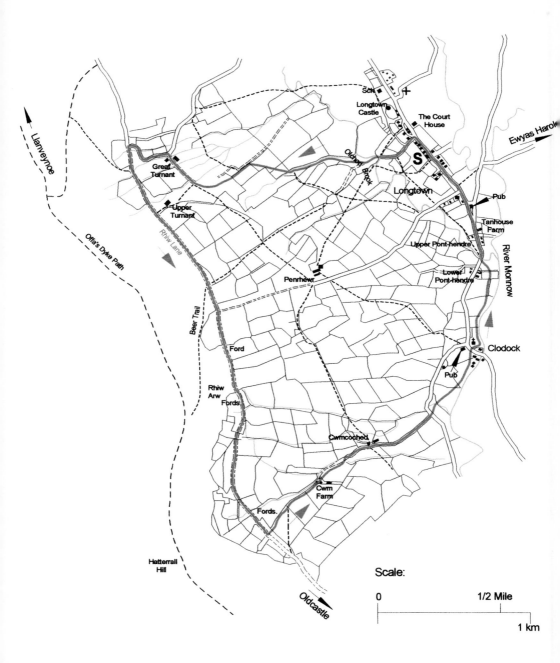

Sch

Longtown
Castle

The Court
House

S

Ewyas Harol

Longtown

Great
Turnant

Olchon Brook

Pub

Upper
Turnant

Tanhouse
Farm

Rhiw Lane

Upper Pont-hendre

River Monnow

Offa's Dyke Path

Penrhew

Lower
Pont-hendre

Beer Trail

Llanveynoe

Ford

Clodock

Pub

Rhiw
Arw
Fords

Cwmcoched

Cwm
Farm

Fords.

Hatterrall
Hill

Oldcastle

Scale:

0   1/2 Mile

1 km

Length	7 miles
OS Map	OL 13
Start	Village Hall at Longtown GR324288
Parking	Village Hall
Refreshments	The Crown Inn (01873 860217), Longtown,
	The Cornwall Arms (01873 860677), Clodock
Public Transport	Very limited bus service

Circular Route

From Longtown Village Hall turn left towards the castle, but before reaching its ruined remains follow the 'no through road' on the left that dips down to ford the Olchon Brook. From the opposite bank a stile on the right is the start of a footpath that leads across three fields, a footbridge and diagonally left through further fields to reach a gate and a green lane. Do not enter the gate, but turn left above the sunken lane heading west until reaching a farm track on the right. This crosses a ford and leads through the farm buildings at Great Turnant to a tarmac lane.

This tarmaced lane from Longtown is followed left around a narrow bend to reach the start of the delightful unsurfaced Rhiw Lane leading sharp left from the junction. Although muddy, uneven and waterlogged in parts, the going does not detract from admiring this lane offering stunning views as it winds its way between stone walls, hedges and across open moor land over the Beer Trail and along the contours of the hills known as the Black Mountains

After following the lane for around two and a half miles, the pleasant green lane is abandoned just after a series of mini fords at the third waymarked path on the left. Cross a well marked stile and descend through fields and a short section of a boggy green lane to Cwm Farm, where a firmer surface leads past another farm at Cwmcoched. From there a tarmac lane leads down to the road and a footpath ahead following the banks of the River Monnow to the church and pub at Clodock.

A short break may be enjoyed at Clodock before continuing through the weathered gravestones in the churchyard to a stone stile. The path initially follows the banks of the Monnow and then veers slightly left towards Longtown. At the road cross the bridge over the Olchon and follow the road signed to Longtown Castle which passes the Tanhouse and the Crown Inn to return to the Village Hall.

This tombstone was found under the nave of this Church in 1917.

It dates from the ninth century and is the oldest known Latin inscription, so far, found in Herefordshire and reads as follows :—

"This tomb holds the remains of the faithful and dear wife of GUINNDAS, who was herself a native of this place."

Ninth century stone in Clodock church

Church and pub at Clodock

Sources

Books
- *Herefordshire Council Unclassified Roads 1935*
- *B Copleston-Crow, Herefordshire Place names 1989*
- *Walks from Llanthony Priory 1997*
- *A Ross, Walking in the Black Mountains 2006*
- *R Palmer, The Folklore of Monmouthshire 1998*
- *J Eisel, & F Bennett, The Pubs of Hay-on-Wye 2005*
- *G Moore, The Parish Church of St. Clydawg nd.*
- *Herefordshire Directories 1851-1941*

Archives
- *Upper Turnant Sale 1919 HRO M5/21/48*
- *Rhiw sale 1878 HRO E59/SP/20*
- *Rhiw sale 1920 HRO M5/36/2*
- *Longtown ROW survey 1952 HRO CD31/8*
- *Llanveynoe ROW survey 1952 HRO CD31/7*

Maps
- *OS 1831, 2006*
- *Longtown Tithe Map 1840*
- *Llanveynoe Tithe Map 1840*

Websites
- *Ewyas Lacy 2009 ewyaslacy.org.uk*
- *Longtown Historical Society Archive www.lhsarchive.org.uk*

98

Tibberton
Court

Todelitch

Swinemoor

Upper Chilson

Bage Mill

Bage

Wormhill

Lower Chilson

Chilson's Orle

Bucknalls Wood

Wormhill Farm

Withies

8

Lower Cublington

Slowell Farm

Town House
Madley

North

Wychyalls Cross

Redhe

Upper Cublington

Castle

Lower Shenmoor

Parsquay Parkway

Marsh House

Barbers Green

Little Brampton

Timberline Wood

Hill Barn

Great Brampton

Webton

Goldstone Common

Bache

Blackhole Barn

Coldwell

Bridan Court
Turners House

Stradel Bridge

Cottage

Hanty Court

Kingston Mill

Brampton Hill

Harfall

Bigsly

Ash Coppice

Arkstone Dunswater

Newbarn Farm

New Barn Wood

Nells Wood

Blackmoor

Kingston Grange
Orl Wood

Thruxton

Well

Dunscot Wood

Cockyett Tump
Newbrook

Whitfield

Whitfield Wood

Farm House

Landerwen

Carey Gate

Lime Quarry

Park Farm

Blackbush

Titles Hill

Lower Jury

Treville Wood

Treville

Enlarged extract from Ordnance Survey First Edition 1 inch to 1 mile map (Old Series) 1831

9

Stone Street, Madley

The stretch of Stone Street from Great Brampton to Blackmoor Farm closely follows the course of the Roman Road leading south from the Roman town of Magna in Kenchester. From Great Brampton the road runs along a straight course, which is a characteristic of Roman roads. It is lightly tarmaced, narrow and enclosed by tall hedges forming a natural archway across the road. Further along the hedges have been trimmed, and due to lack of use, grass grows along the centre of this road now classified as a byway.

From the Hay road the byway takes on a different appearance. It forms a typical green lane of carriageway width, unsurfaced and sunken in parts as it winds across Brampton Hill. Steep ivy covered banks are topped with hedges of birch, holly and yew which form an attractive tunnel on the ascent. Sections are muddy showing some stoning or paving in the past and a double row of banks are visible in places. From the property at the top of Brampton Hill the lane descends along a gravelled track which curves down to Crossway. These features suggest either an earlier route reused by the Romans or a possible medieval diversion from the straighter course of the Roman period as shown on a map of 1981 produced by Hereford and Worcester Council.

History
Roman roads have always fascinated archaeologists and historians who have excavated, investigated and researched their routes across the countryside. According to the experts Stone Street connected Chester with Caerleon passing through two towns which lie within the present county of Herefordshire – Leintwardine and Kenchester. Over the years the section from Kenchester to Abbey Dore has been investigated by archaeologists and the county based Woolhope Club. Various finds have been discovered and identified from the Romano British period including two lamps, an urn, boulders 'of the type used in the construction of Stone Street' and 'part of an iron horseshoe found on the Roman road near Abbey Dore – identified by the British Museum as being probably 4th to 6th century AD'.

Stony Street 1780, Madley

Madley Assize Roll 1292

Use of the name street often signifies a road of Roman origin, and it is likely that the 'Stanisstret' stretching to a ' higway called Portwey' in 1250 refers to the present day Stone Street. In 1780 it was shown as 'Stony Street a Roman Road', Stone Street in 1815, Stony Street in 1817, Stoneway in 1835, Stoney Street in 1843 and Stone Street from 1888. Two farms along the road are called Stoney Street and Street House – which was offered for sale in 1924 as a 'Brick-built, well planned, superior, Detached Double-fronted detached residence' with 18 acres and common rights on Orling Meadow fronting the Roman road.

Characteristic features of Roman roads are the agger, a gentle cambered causeway, with kerbs and side ditches, but in Herefordshire these features appear to have been modified. Traces of agger have been identified along the course of Stone Street including the 'crossing of the Wye at Huff Pool, Old Weir'. Roman roads are known to follow a straight alignments, but often adapted earlier more sinuous routes, such as the green lane across Brampton Hill 'reputed to be a Roman road', and described in the early 13th century as 'Portam de Stradell' indicating the gate of Straddle at Brampton Hill.

The wood at Brampton Hill is a' hill top wood with many indicator species of ancient woodland', in 1840 there were compartments of rough pasture and arable and in 1929 the woodland consisted of oak and ash with coppices of ash, hazel and black sally. By 2002 most parts had been cleared and planted with larch, chestnut and oak, and quarry workings and boundary banks were identified in the north-east strip of woodland. It was formerly part of the Guy's Hospital Estate, whose green notices are still visible although taken over by the Duchy of Cornwall around 2000.

At Crossway Cottage Stone Street continues in a south-westerly direction from the junction to Kerry's Gate, where a minor road signed to Cockyard leads to Wormbridge and Kilpeck. It was possibly along this route that in 1292 the 'Abbot of Dore made a certain encroachment over the road that leads from Brampton towards Kilpeck and Wormbridge where people were accustomed to cross with wagons and horse carts where no one can cross'. The abbot said the 'road is not a kings highway for droving, for carts and wagons nor a common path for riders and pedestrians', but the jurors ordered the sheriff 'to make the road open from the obstruction.'

Stone Street passes Blackmoor Farm situated on the stream that runs through the Grey Valley. Blackmoor has been recorded as an Historic Farm by the Herefordshire Historic Farmsteads project, but it is difficult to

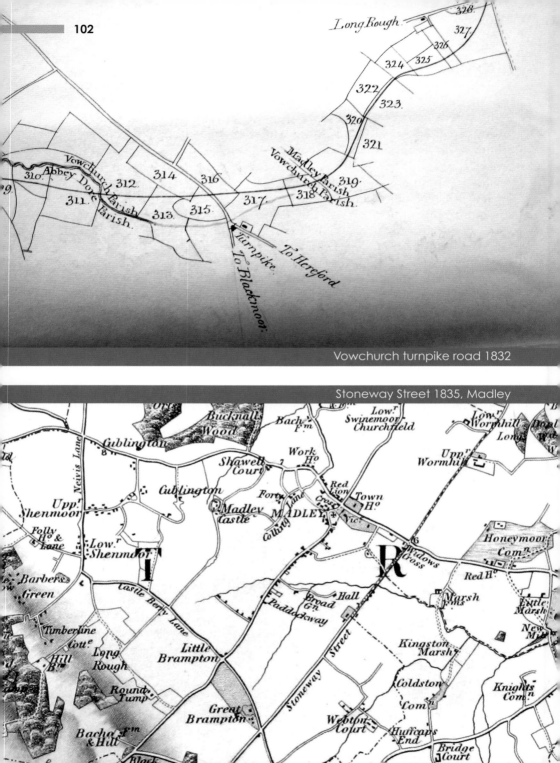

Vowchurch turnpike road 1832

Stoneway Street 1835, Madley

see the building from Stone Street due to modern barns obscuring the view. Blackmoor enjoys an interesting history, as it was a grange which belonged to the Cistercian monks at Abbey Dore. Various earthworks have been discovered which suggest a moated site 'perhaps for protection of wandering animals'.

A toll bar once stood at the junction of roads from Newbarns and Hay-on-Wye alongside the B4348 which was turnpiked in 1810, with a 'Proposed new Line' suggested in 1832. From this junction a pleasant footpath leads north through fields and woodland of the Tyberton Section of the former Guy's Hospital Estate. In 1961 the fields were part of Holsty Farm in Vowchurch and the woods of 527 acres included Lady Coppice and Timberline which contained standing timber of oak, ash, sweet chestnut, chestnut, Wych elm, larch, conifers and poplars.

From Lower Shenmore the road shown as Neivis Lane, in 1835, leads through this quiet hamlet where a network of paths and byways lead in all directions. Over a hundred years ago at Shenmore there was a shop, a brick maker, a carpenter, a wheelwright and a Primitive Methodist Chapel. The Chapel House was originally two cottages, and sold as a smallholding with two acres in 1921. A byway leads to Cublington where paths and green lanes head south to Castle Berry Lane, the former smithy at Little Brampton, and Great Brampton House which according to its sale particulars of 1929 was only built 'in the Italian style' during the 1890s, which must have been a rebuild.

Exploring Stone Street

A glance at any map, dating from the late 18th century, will immediately reveal the line of the Roman Road known as Stone Street leading through Madley and Abbey Dore. From Great Brampton this Roman road can be pleasantly explored along a quiet byway before crossing the Hay road, where the route continues as an unsurfaced green lane winding across Brampton Hill Wood to the Grey Valley in the adjoining parish of Abbey Dore. A further straight section passes Blackmoor Farm and leads to the start of a scenic return via Newbarns Farm, Lady Coppice, Timberline Wood, Shenmore and Cublington.

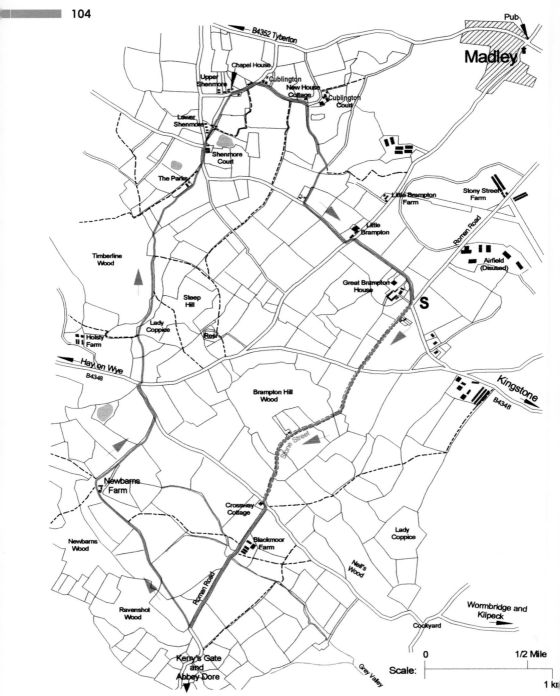

Length	**7.5 miles**
OS Map	**Explorer 189/OL13**
Start	**Great Brampton GR412368**
Parking	**Roman Road north of Great Brampton**
Refreshments	**Red Lion at Madley (01981 250600)**
Public Transport	**449 bus (Yeomans) Hereford to Brampton**

Circular Route

From Great Brampton House follow the line of the Roman Road which heads south along the tarmaced byway. It crosses the Hay-on-Wye road then winds and climbs across Brampton Hill before descending to an almost hidden cottage and minor road junction at Crossway in Abbey Dore. Follow the road signed to Kerrys Gate and Bacton which is clearly marked as Stone Street on the current Ordnance Survey map.

After passing the intriguing building at Blackmoor Farm, turn right over a stile inscribed AD13 (the footpath number) where the field path leads through sheep pastures below the sullen woods of Newbarns to Newbarns Farm. There is a junction of footpaths at this farm, so be careful to follow the one leading right from the far side of the farm. It traverses a field to join the drive offering views of the Black Mountains before reaching the road.

Follow this minor road to the left, re-cross the Hay road and cross a signed stile opposite. The waymarked path is easily followed through fields to a stile and along a pretty woodland path through Lady Coppice and the edge of Timberline Wood. At a clearing the footpath crosses a field and from the next stile veers diagonally right as waymarked to the right hand side of a property named The Parks, where within a few hundred yards the road is reached at Shenmore.

The final stretch follows the road in a northerly direction past Shenmore Court to a stile on the right, where the way ahead leads pleasantly through fields passing a pool of water before reaching Upper Shenmore opposite Chapel House. Follow the road to the right, ignore the signed path but take the unsigned byway on the right at Cublington. This green lane winds around past New House Cottage to a footpath on the right which leads across meadows to a byway, which is followed south to the road leading left to Little and Great Brampton in Madley.

View of the Grey Valley, Abbeydore

Stone Street 2010, Madley

Sources

Books and Journals
- *J H Turner, Herefordshire Countryside Treasures 1981*
- *B Smith, Herefordshire Maps 2004*
- *H Hurley, The Old Roads of South Herefordshire, 2nd ed 2007*
- *B Coplestone-Crow, Herefordshire Place Names 2nd ed 2009*
- *R Shoesmith and R Richardson, Dore Abbey 1997*
- *Herefordshire Directories 1858, 1876, 1902*
- *TWNFC 1967*

Archives
- *Release HCA 1104*
- *Great Brampton Sale 1929 HRO M5/24/9*
- *Assize Rolls 1292 TNA JUST1/303*
- *Translation of JUST1/303 by David Lovelace*
- *Street House Farm sale 1924 HRO M5/23/8*
- *Guy's Hospital Estate sale 1961*
- *Great Brampton House sale 1929 HRO M5/24/9*
- *Chapel House sale 1921 HRO M5/24/5*
- *Proposed new line of road 1832 HRO Q/RWt27*

Maps
- *OSD 1815, OS 1888, 2006*
- *Taylor 1754, Taylor 1780 HCA 4768*
- *Bryant 1835*
- *Price 1817*
- *Abbey Dore Tithe Map 1840*
- *Madley Tithe Map 1843*

Websites
- *Herefordshire Sites and Monuments www.smr.herefordshire.gov.uk*
- *Archenfield Archaeology www.archenfield.com*
- *Genuki www.genuki.org.uk/search*

Church coppice
River Arrow
Knoll
New fire
Pen lang
Lower Hengoed
Vals Place
Huntington school
Burnt Hengoed
Brysi Bridge
Little Folly
Middle Hengoed
Renwild
Up. Hengoed
Hales Mill
Wern
Black coch
Quarrybank
Penir draw
Gwen y bwch
Turret
Pen lake
Quarry house
Great Folly
Bwlchwm Hall
Little Gaer
Fern H.
Michaelchurch Hill
Wain wen
Milton Mill
Gaer
Cwm...
Castle Coppel
Lower Corner
Newchurch
Michael Church
Summer Pole
Pen y gwraddel
Lan pica
Wern Wood
Tre newydd
Cross way
Llanb
Red burrow
Little Wern
High Grove
Mill
Grove
Little Lane House
Lane
Mountain
The red lane
Yew Tree Hall
Launstons
Brilley
Corast
Bush
Pentre miley
Inn House
Pentre
Brilley C
Pentre r gove
Brilley Court
Pen y castell
Wern
Lower Bridge Court
Knap
Instell
Bridge court
Wood House
Crowthers Pool
Penlwyn
Bullydias
Pound
Green Wood
Pant
Pen brilley
Sunny bank
Cwm cethin
Maes y magien
Bank of pleasure
17
Cae noyald
Cae thugin
Wood spring
Cwm gwilim
Cwm r alu
Whitney Bridge
Common
Whitney
Bettws Chapel
Rhyd spence
Lane House
Up. House
Pen y wern
Ferry
Tram Road
Pen r heol
Lower Cabalva
Sheepcot
Pen twyn
Bettws
Cwm bank
Clifford Place
Lacksto
Whitlow Mill
Cwm pelved
Upper Cabalva
The Farm
Cross foot
Stocking
Tall Trees
Tun y wern
Castle
Ton
Priory Wood
Clifford Park
The Cottage
Brenault
Ton Wood
Clifford
Court Evan Gwun
Grove Wood
Green Lane
Pen y Park
Cwm buddog
Priory

Enlarged extract from Ordnance Survey First Edition 1 inch to 1 mile map (Old Series) 1831

10

Red Lane, Brilley

The section of the Red Lane that leads from Milton Hill to Little Mountain along the Welsh border is of ancient origin and assumed to form part of a Roman route. There is little evidence of a paved surface along the wide green lane, but archaeologists did find traces of agger and metaling, although not 'very Roman in appearance'. The Red Lane is approached by a track signed as a 'Public Road' and as 'Unsuitable for Motor Vehicles' which leads between hedges to a bridle gate and the start of The Red Lane as indicated on the 1814 survey. From the bridle gate the little-used green lane leads between boundary banks and hedges with surprisingly wide verges suggesting its use as a drove road.

From the extremely wide grass surfaced lane views of the Radnorshire Hills emerge, and as it heads west the Red Lane features a growth of trees and shrubs along its verges which form an attractive woodland way leading to the present day Offa's Dyke Path. This waymarked route leads south along a narrower lane leading between thick banks of hedges and is named Red Lane on recent Ordnance Surveys. Before reaching a crossways the lane is partly tarmaced but continues ahead as a green lane of great width lined with hedges and remnants of stone walls along its western side.

History

Brilley in northwest Herefordshire is a remote and thinly populated parish with a pattern of early winding roads, lanes and footpaths linking its farms and settlements. The landscape of fields and woods are intersected by deep-banked brooks flowing down to the Wye from the higher slopes below Brilley Mountain and Milton Hill. The Red Lane is one of many green lanes in the area that is unsurfaced, of carriageway width and of historical importance. As an assumed Roman route the Red Lane would have formed part of a road from Mortimer's Cross across Herefordshire and Radnorshire to the Roman fort at Castell Collen northwest of Llandrindod Wells.

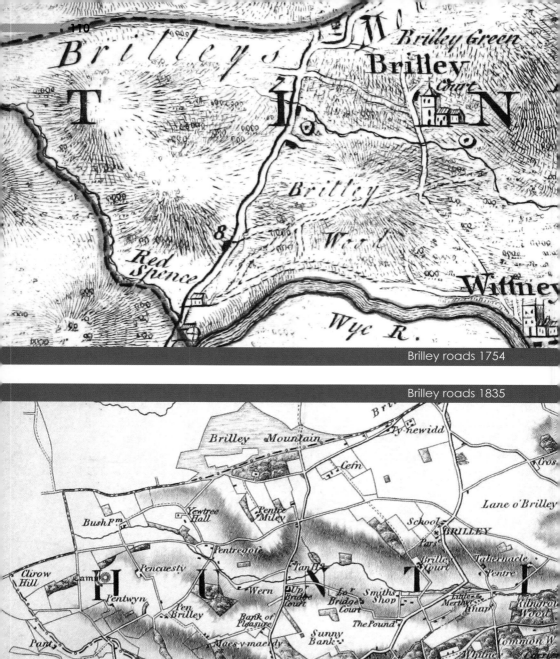

Brilley roads 1754

Brilley roads 1835

The lane has been in continuous use since these early times and from its width and grassy verges there is physical evidence to suggest that it was used as a drove way. Since the Middle Ages herds of cattle from Wales were driven to the English markets, and it is known that from the 18th century 'thirty thousand black cattle from the summer and autumn fairs of Wales went, every year in huge herds through Herefordshire, towards south-east England, choosing, like the Scotch cattle, the bye-lanes in order to avoid the turnpike tolls'. Travelling at 12 to 16 miles a day the cattle and the drovers' sturdy ponies would have needed to be watered, rested and grazed along routes offering these facilities.

The Red Lane recorded in 1831 running east west would have been used by drovers bringing cattle via Glascwm, Newchurch Hill and Little Mountain then along Red Lane towards Kington, where other drove roads met. A detour 'mainly along traditional tracks and by short-cuts across open moorland' would have been sought to avoid the toll road from Brilley Mountain to Kington, which was turnpiked in 1754 as shown on Taylor's map. By 1833 the Red Lane would have been at its busiest when droving reached its peak before the opening of the railways, which took over the trade from the second half of the 19th century. The lane possible fell into disuse by 1904, was not listed in 1936 and by 1952 was still known as the 'Red Lane on Parish Boundary'.

Sometime during the latter half of the 20th century the marking of the Red Lane was shifted to the north south branch which features all the characteristics of a drove road as it winds down towards Rhydspence and its known river crossing. The cattle were driven via Colva and Newchurch in Radnorshire and down the Red Lane to meet the steep pitch to the inn and the crossing over the Wye also used by other 'drovers coming through Rhydspence, from Clyro, Painscastle and Erwood'. The name Rhydspence is derived from the Welsh 'rhyd' meaning ford, and it has been suggested that the 'pence' refers to an amount paid for fields let 'to the drovers to rest and revitalise' their livestock. The Red Lane probably acquired an anglicised form of rhyd to mean ford lane.

The timber-framed Rhydspence Inn dates from the 16th century with many interesting features including a two-storey porch, a stone mounting block and some mullion windows. It stands right on the boundary of England and Wales and its history has been closely associated with the drovers when it was an ale and cider house known alternatively as the 'Cattle Inn'. It was from the 1950s that the old inn blossomed into an

Rhydspence Inn, Brilley

Rhydspense Plantation 1919, Brilley

hotel and restaurant. A creaking cider press and the Drover's Barn are the only noticeable reminders of Rhydspence's earlier history.

Apart from the Rhydspence Inn there had been other licensed premises in the Brilley area which have long since closed their doors. The former New Inn was a 'fully licensed public house' in 1883, the Red Lion had enjoyed a 'profitable trade ' in 1906 whereas the Travellers Rest and Green Arms of 1858 were short lived. These together with the earlier Summer Pole Inn of 1835 would have served a working community of farmers, stone masons, sawyers, blacksmiths, shopkeepers, carpenters and the travelling drovers during the 19th century.

Exploring Red Lane

A superb route follows green lanes and field paths in the parish of Brilley on the Radnorshire border in the northwest of Herefordshire where Welsh place-names serve as a reminder of its close association with its neighbouring country. Starting from the village church the route almost immediately follows a series of green lanes, the first being wet and muddy in places before improving and ascending below the open slopes of Milton Hill to the start of 'The Red Lane'. At its junction with the present day Offa's Dyke Path it heads south towards Rhydspence and descends a pleasant field path to the Wye. From the Rhydspence Inn a meandering route leads through woods, fields and a final green lane before returning to the start.

Length	8.5 miles
OS Map	Explorer 201
Start	Brilley Church GR261494
Parking	Small parking area by church (donation to church funds)
Refreshments	Rhydspence Inn (01497 831262), Brilley
Public Transport	Infrequent bus service from Kington

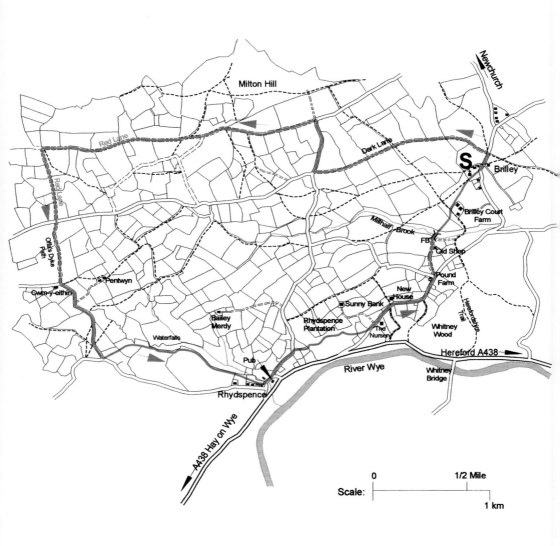

Scale:

0	1/2 Mile
	1 km

Circular Route

From Brilley church gate follow the road past the Old School House and Old Forge and within a few hundred yards turn left along a signed green lane once known as Dark Lane. It is rutted and muddy but improves before reaching a crossways. The tarmac lane on the right ascends to another crossways where a higher level green lane signed as a Public Road leads to the west below Milton Hill, which rises to nearly 1,000 feet.

At a fork, keep right through a bridle gate along the boundary between Herefordshire in England and Radnorshire in Wales. This stretch, clearly recorded in 1831 as 'The Red Lane', is remote and wild offering fine views of the bracken clad hills of Radnorshire. From the Offa's Dyke Path signpost the Red Lane continues south down the signed route and becomes tarmaced, but after crossing a road regains its green surface and former width.

At Cwm-yr-eithin the road ahead descends to a junction identified by a tall modern chimney. The footpath opposite leads through fields and above a steep sided brook as directed by the numerous Welsh waymarks. A delightful grey-stone cottage is passed as a steeper descent is made into Herefordshire at Rhydspence. Unfortunately the attractive old inn does not serve out of strict opening times, but the mounting block makes a suitable resting place. From the inn follow the narrow tarmac lane signed to Brynafal and a short way up the hill cross a stile on the right where a recently waymarked path zigzags through Rhydspence Plantation, with views of the Wye and Whitney Bridge spied through the trees.

The path joins the road at The Nursery where a gradual climb passes New House and the former New Inn before reaching Pound Farm. Beyond the farm a signed path follows the final green lane leading to a cottage called the Old Shop, once used as a carpenter's shop. The way continues over a narrow footbridge crossing the Millhalf Brook and through fields skirting Brilley Court Farm. With an assortment of waymarked paths be sure to choose the one beside the open barn to a hidden gate with a framed view of Brilley church across the last field.

View from Red Lane, Brilley

Red Lane 2009

Sources

Books and Journals

- *J Jones, Offa's Dyke Path 1976*
- *H Hurley, The Old Roads of South Herefordshire 2nd ed 2007*
- *R Palmer, The Folklore of Radnorshire 2001*
- *P Hindle, Roads and Tracks 2001*
- *R Shoesmith & R Barrett, The Pubs of Leominster & Kington 2000*
- *Herefordshire Directories 1858 - 1941*
- *J Sinclair & W Fenn, A Brilley Walk 2002*
- *R Moore-Colyer, Welsh Cattle Drovers 2002*
- *HAN 47, 1987*
- *Radnorshire Society Transactions 1984*
- *Herefordshire Council Unclassified Roads 1936*

Archives

- *Brilley ROW 1952, HRO CD31/18*
- *Red Lion sale particulars 1906 HRO M5/16/51*
- *New Inn sale particulars 1883, 1920 HRO AD57/26*
- *Kington Road Act 1756 HCL*
- *Rhydspence Plantation sale 1919, HRO M5/5/75*

Maps

- *OSD 1814, OS 1831, 1833, 1904, 2006*
- *Herefordshire County Road Map 1985*
- *Bryant 1835*
- *Taylor 1754*

Websites

- *Herefordshire Sites and Monuments www.smr.herefordshire.gov.uk*
- *About Brilley www.brilley.co.uk*
- *Clwyd-Powys Archaeological Trust www.cpat.org.uk*
- *Rhydspence Inn www.rhydspence-inn.co.uk*

Back Brook

Rodd

Nash

T.P.

Rodd Hurst

Ashley

Camp

Harton

Highland

Rodd Wood

Weobley Ash

Broadford

Little Brampton

Brampton Head

Green Lane

Butcher Wood

Burnt House

Shutting Wood

Turning Way

Butcher

Upper Mowley

Lower Mowley

T.G.

Priory Leasow

Mowle

Gorsty Dole

Titley

Oat Croft

Titley Court

Strangwood

Dog Kennel

Lywood

Forge

Shaw

Roses

The V

Golden Bank

Arrow

Strangwood

Flintsham

Hunton

Tumulus

Coppet Wood

w pits

Cabbage Hall

Cottas Dale

Lords Mill

Rushock

Wych

Lower Downfield

Nextend

Whittern

Mill Farm

Sunset

Bullocks Mill

Brook

Parkstile

Lion Hall

GTON

Coppice

Castle

The Heath

Naidon

Weir

Co

3

leasow

Enlarged extract from Ordnance Survey First Edition 1 inch to 1 mile map (Old Series) 1831

11

Green Lane, Titley

The Green Lane follows the boundary between the parishes of Titley and Rodd, Nash and Little Brampton which probably indicates it is of ancient origin. Although of carriageway width it is wider in places with a grass surface and evidence of having been paved. Banks, thick hedges and a summer growth of bracken and briars enclose the lane which runs along a ridge between Green Lane Farm and the barn at Burnt House. Although forming a section of the Mortimer Way and open to all traffic there are few signs of hoof, boot and tyre marks.

In the past the Green Lane was obviously of some importance as a network of lanes and paths join the lane from various directions including a footpath from Burnt House described in 1952 as leading to a 'disused wagon way', now used as part of the Titley Loop Walk, and other paths lead in a northerly direction to the Turnpike Cottage at Nash. The two unclassified roads recorded in 1935 as leading to the 'Stag, Titley' over a distance of just over one mile and the other of around half a mile to Rodd Hurst are still in use.

History

In the mid 19th century Titley was recorded as 'a picturesque parish and village, with a railway station on the Leominster and Kington railway, which is also the junction of the newly-constructed lines from Kington to Eardisley, and from Kington to Presteigne. The station, although called "Titley", is locally situate in the parish of Lyonshall, being distant about 1 mile south of Titley village. The river Arrow and the main road from Kington to Presteigne run through the parish, which is distant three miles N.E. of Kington'. This road replaced an earlier 18th-century toll road of six miles from Presteigne which crossed the Green Lane at Burnt House and followed a route past Gorsty Dole and Golden Bank to Rushock before it led to Kington.

This route must have been turnpiked by the Presteigne and Mortimer's Cross Trust in 1754 as it is shown on Taylor's county map of that date, and not by the Kington Turnpike Trust as previously suggested because it

AJTI/31

Mr Gething Kingsland Dr to William Griffiths

	£ s d
Filling Routs	0 5 0
Onloding and Breeking 2 load of stone	0 1 10
Cleaning a Ditch 12 Pearch at 2 d Peh	0 2 0
Scraping 16 at one d a Peh	0 1 4
	10 2

Recd the Contents of Mr Ward by me William Griffiths

Titley road repairs 1825

Titley roads 1754

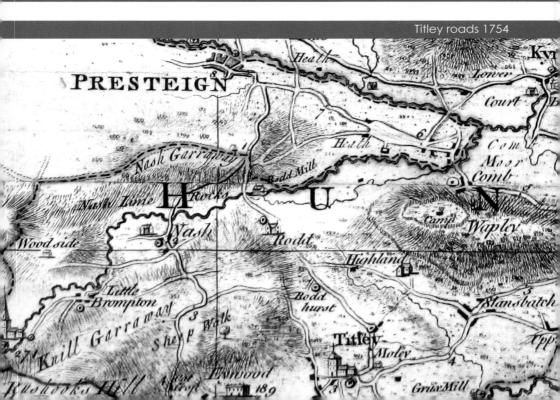

does not relate to the road 'through Titley and Stansbatch under the side of Wapley Hill to Staple Bar' described in the 1756 road act. Although these earlier routes 'seem insignificant to our modern eye, they formed essential parts of the web of routes which the Trust souaThe roads and bridges in Titley during the 18th century were continually recorded as 'out of repair', 'in ruinous condition' and 'in great need of repair'. In 1804 there was concern about 'keeping up 2 bridges' and in 1825 stone was broken for 'filling the roads' and the ditches were cleaned. Despite improvements the roads around Kington were so bad that the following incident occurred in 1848: 'the leader of a team of sixteen horses bringing stones for the road fell into the mud and it required the strength of the remaining fifteen to get him out, so unrecognisable as a horse that the people of Kington came to see the spectacle'.

The ridgeway route along Green Lane may be of ancient origin, linking Hergest Ridge to the Iron Age hill-fort on Wapley Hill. Green Lane Farm lies close to the site of an Iron Age farmstead with evidence of banks and ditches identified by archaeologists. They have also recorded the present day Green Lane Farm as an Historic Farm and the 'Green Lane holloway' from the farm to Burnt House as 'quite wide in places' and queried as a drove road. In 1952 the Green Lane at Titley was defined as a footpath from Green Lane Farm following the parish boundary to the south west corner of Stocking Wood where it was overgrown with bracken.

In 1725 William Thomas was recorded as a churchwarden at the Burnt House, a 17th century stone building of two storeys, inhabited by Mrs West in 1867, and described as being in a 'fairly good' condition in 1934 but probably unoccupied since then. Today the stone barn is the only remaining feature of this farmstead where further lanes lead to Gorsty Dole and Oakcroft Farm, which were offered for sale as part of the 'outlying portions of the Brampton Bryan Estate' in 1912. A pleasant green lane passes the isolated buildings of the Dog Kennel Homestead of 1843 and continues down to Rushock where footpaths are joined.

The only other green lane on this walk is reached from the Square at Titley, where a footpath signed as the Herefordshire Trail leads through the grounds of Eywood which 'display a great diversity of scenery, and are ornamented with some fine plantations' to an enclosed narrow lane. Clearly shown on maps of 1815 it must be a remnant of a longer route through the estate. Eyewood was formerly a residence of the Harleys,

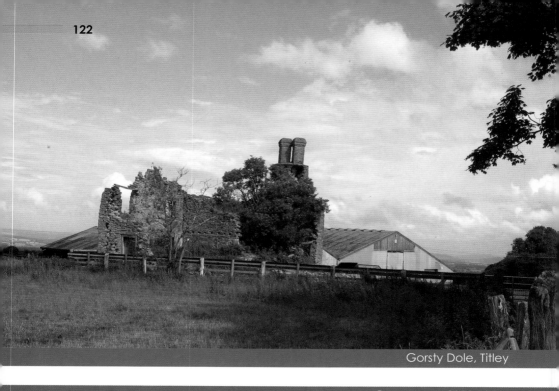

Gorsty Dole, Titley

Green Lane 2009, Titley

but after being sold in the late 19th century it passed through various ownerships before the estate was broken up and the mansion demolished in the mid 20th century.

This final green lane leads to within yards of the Stagg Inn at Titley, the perfect place for rest and refreshment. According to the pub's history the Stagg was 'built at the meeting point of 2 drove roads and is part medieval, part early Victorian with a bit of the 1970s. Today it is rustic in feel with a small bar housing a collection of 200 pub jugs and some very friendly gossiping locals' and although there are 3 dining rooms many diners prefer to eat in the bar. From 1802 the Stagg was known as the Balance Inn until 1833, when the following was recorded in the diaries written by Lady Greenly of Titley Court 'Mr. Banks came and held a court for the surrender of the Balance Inn (afterwards the Stag's Head) to my father, who had bought it of William Powell for £550. I now fronted the Stag's Head with brick, and made other alterations there.'

Exploring Green Lane, Titley

The Green Lane at Titley is named on the present Ordnance Survey and shown as a restricted byway forming part of the Mortimer Trail, a 30 mile waymarked route leading from Kington to Ludlow. The section along the Green Lane is open to walkers, riders and cyclists in the north west corner of Herefordshire, where many bridleways and other routes with public access have been recently opened. From Titley the route ascends the Mortimer Trail to the Green Lane leading to bracken clad slopes offering panoramic views above Gorsty Dole. Further lanes and paths descend along a former turnpike road and through Rushock to the River Arrow, where a level route along the river and dismantled railway add interest before returning to Titley.

Length	**9 miles**
OS Map	**Explorer 201**
Start	**Stagg Inn, Titley**
Parking	**Village hall GR329599, Titley**
Refreshments	**Stagg Inn (01544 230221), Titley**

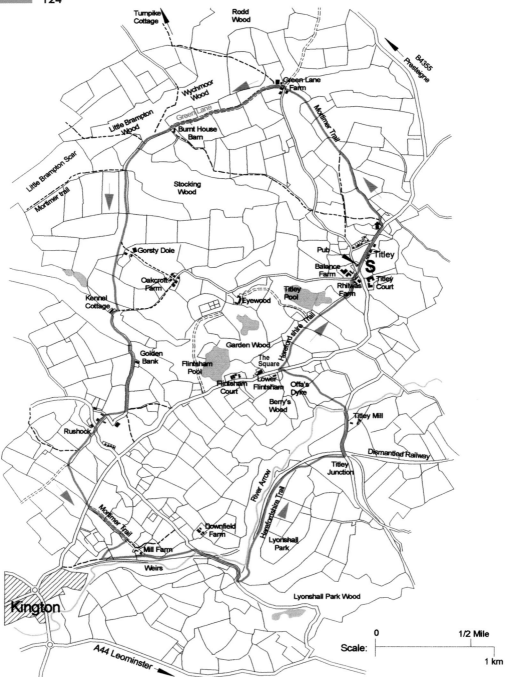

Scale:

0		1/2 Mile
		1 km

Circular Route

From the Stagg follow the road towards Presteigne and beyond the church, dedicated to St. Peter, follow the Mortimer Trail on the left, which climbs through fields to Green Lane Farm and a junction of ways. Take care to follow the unsurfaced Green Lane leading west and passing a stone barn at Burnt House. From there the waymarked trail leads through open hillside and fields to a signed footpath leading south to Gorsty Dole with its stark ruin.

Before reaching the farm buildings of Gorsty Dole a field path on the right descends across stiles to join a green lane at Kennel Cottage. This lane, a byway and cycleway, is followed to the right as it gradually descends before becoming tarmaced. After passing a solitary house at Golden Bank a footpath on the right at Rushock rejoins the Mortimer Trail, which is followed through farmland and across the Presteigne road to join a riverside path along the Arrow now part of the Herefordshire Trail.

The trail keeps to the north side of the river and the dismantled remains of the Leominster to Kington Railway and passes behind Mill Farm to join a minor road leading over the Arrow, where a weir may be glimpsed from the attractive stone bridge. Several picturesque buildings and a former corn mill in Lyonshill parish are prettily situated before a signed bridleway leads through woodland above the river and railway.

At Titley Junction the station, carriages and railway line are being restored, but as it is in private ownership keep to the waymarked trail until reaching the road leading north to Titley. After re crossing the Arrow the Herefordshire Trail follows a zigzag course over the earth works of Offa's Dyke, across the Presteigne road at the Square and gently uphill through sheep grazed meadows to a green lane leading to Titley and the Stagg Inn.

Titley church

Stagg Inn, Titley

Sources

Books and Journals

- *Parks & Countryside Service, The Mortimer Trail 2002*
- *Hereford R A, The Herefordshire Trail 2004*
- *Herefordshire Council, The Titley Loop Walk 2002*
- *Herefordshire Council, Unclassified Roads 1935*
- *Herefordshire Directories 1867, 1876*
- *W Howse, Radnorshire 1949*
- *RCHM Vol III 1934*
- *D Whitehead, A Survey of Historic Parks & Gardens 2001*
- *V Harrison, Kington nd HCL*
- *R Shoesmith & R Barrett, The Pubs of Leominster & Kington 2000*
- *J Sinclair & R Fenn, The New Kington History 1995*
- *K Parker, A History of Presteigne 1997*
- *Herefordshire Archaeology, The Arrow Valley 2003*
- *D Viner, The Kington Turnpike Trust TWNFC 1987*

Archives

- *Titley ROW Survey 1952 HRO CD31/20*
- *Kington Road Act 1756 HCL*
- *Brampton Bryan Sale 1912 NMR printed*
- *Greenly Diaries HRO D6/2*
- *Road and Bridge Repairs 1825 HRO AJ97/31*
- *QS records 1752 - 1804 HRO*
- *Titley Parish Records HRO*

Maps

- *Price 1817*
- *Titley Tithe Map 1843*
- *Taylor 1754*
- *OSD 1815, OS 1831, 1888, 2006*

Websites

- *Titley Junction www.titleyjunctionstation.co.uk*
- *Herefordshire Sites and Monuments www.smr.herefordshire.gov.uk*

Illustrations

Herefordshire Record Office
20 upper Bryant map 1835
22 lower Harewood survey 1833 AW22/1
30 lower Wellington Court sale 1883 N78/45
50 upper Enrolment books Panniers Lane Gate 1875 Q/CE/1
52 upper Buckenhill Estate sale 1856 C97/3
52 lower Saltmarsh estate map 1841 B54/1
60 lower Fish Inn sale 1701 L34/9/13
80 upper Inclosure Act 1806 Bl52/59
82 upper Perambulations 1834 BO9/1
90 upper Marquess of Abergavenny sale 1920 M5/36/2
102 upper New line of turnpike road 1832 Q/RWt/27
102 lower Bryant map 1835
110 upper Taylor map 1754
110 lower Bryant map 1835
112 lower Rhydspence Plantation sale 1919 M5/5/75
120 upper Titley Road repairs 1825 AJ37/91
120 lower Taylor map 1754

Herefordshire Archaeological Newsletter
10 lower R E Kay Glis Farm No 36 1979

Hereford City Library
18 lower Bredwardine Turnpike tolls 1792
22 upper Holme Lacy Estate sale 1909
60 upper Ledbury Road Act 1721
62 upper Ledbury by Webb 1850s
62 lower Scrapbook containing riots 1735
70 lower Hereford Journal 1794, 1824

Hereford Cathedral Library – Dean and Chapter of Hereford Cathedral
70 upper Court Farm lease 1728 5065/2
100 upper Taylor map of Cublington 1780 4324

Landscape Origins of the Wye Valley
12 upper Ordnance survey 1888
12 lower Red Rail excavation 2005
24 upper Llanfrother Lane 2006
40 upper Ordnance survey 1888

Wellington History Society
32 lower Bridge Lane 1905

Bromyard History Society
50 lower Photograph of Panniers Gate nd P4

The National Archives
30 upper Wellington Assize roll 1293 JUST1/302 20EdI
80 lower Hope Mansell Inquisition 1281 C143/5 9EdI
100 lower Madley Assize roll 1292 JUST1/303m60v

Ron Shoesmith
16 upper Packhorse Inn nd

All other illustrations from the author's collection

Index

View from Ridge Hill